Motiv

Philip Whiteley

- Fast track route to motivating individuals and teams

- Covers the key areas of motivation, from the development of academic theories and celebrated workplace experiments to the new world of restructuring and job insecurity

- Examples and lessons from some of the world's most successful businesses, including LVMH and BP, and ideas from the smartest thinkers, including Abraham Maslow, Douglas McGregor, W Edwards Deming, Lynda Gratton, Fons Trompenaars and Meredith Belbin

- Includes a glossary of key concepts and a comprehensive resources guide

PEOPLE

09.07

>>EXPRESS EXEC.COM<<

essential management thinking at your fingertips

First published 2002 by
Capstone Publishing (A Wiley Company)
8 Newtec Place
Magdalen Road
Oxford OX4 1RE
United Kingdom
http://www.capstoneideas.com

CIP catalogue records for this book are available from the British Library and the
US Library of Congress

ISBN 1-84112-209-2

Printed and bound in Great Britain

This book is printed on acid-free paper

Contents

Introduction to ExpressExec

ExpressExec is 3 million words of the latest management thinking compiled into 10 modules. Each module contains 10 individual titles forming a comprehensive resource of current business practice written by leading practitioners in their field. From brand management to balanced scorecard, ExpressExec enables you to grasp the key concepts behind each subject and implement the theory immediately. Each of the 100 titles is available in print and electronic formats.

Through the ExpressExec.com Website you will discover that you can access the complete resource in a number of ways:

» printed books or e-books;
» e-content – PDF or XML (for licensed syndication) adding value to an intranet or Internet site;
» a corporate e-learning/knowledge management solution providing a cost-effective platform for developing skills and sharing knowledge within an organization;
» bespoke delivery – tailored solutions to solve your need.

Why not visit www.expressexec.com and register for free key management briefings, a monthly newsletter and interactive skills checklists. Share your ideas about ExpressExec and your thoughts about business today.

Please contact elound@wiley-capstone.co.uk for more information.

Introduction to Motivation

» All employees are human, from the chief executive to the call center staff members.

» Research now indicates a correlation between motivation and business performance.

» New thinkers tie in the organizational and human needs, building on a century's worth of psychological study.

Executives from the different managerial disciplines will always argue as to which is the most important. Strategists say positioning is fundamental; marketers that understanding the customer and pitching the brand is the source of all profits; financial controllers will point to the disasters that follow failure to get to grips with their discipline; and technologists will point to the continual transformations in communications technology that change ways of doing business.

There is one thing that the chief executive, the director of marketing, the director of finance and the chief information officer have in common, however: they are all people. What is more, they are all employees, no less than the sales and administration staff or those on the factory floor or call center. And people work best when they are motivated to give of their best.

An increasing body of research is starting to show a strong correlation between the level of motivation in the workforce and performance as measured on the bottom line. Evidence of clear cause and effect is problematic, given the sheer number of variables determining employee well-being and motivation; but the strong correlation demands attention. It appears in large companies and small; in different cultures; and in studies carried out both by academics and by consultancies. (For a summary of some of these research studies, with links for further reading, see the section ''Links between motivation and the bottom line,'' in Chapter 9.)

One of the principal management thinkers to study these links is Jeffrey Pfeffer, professor of organizational behavior at Stanford University in the United States, whose book *The Human Equation: Building Profits by Putting People First* argues that people matter because they are the organization and embody its aims. The way in which people are treated cannot be divorced from general management, and companies fail where staff are competing against each other.

The results should not be surprising. Since the early 1990s the majority of the value of companies has comprised intangible assets, and these intangible factors – maintaining the brand, teamworking, research and development capacity, and so on – are the reflection of the combined efforts of the people.

There is also a century's worth of psychological study into the nature of human needs, drives, and desires. Some theories, such as Abraham

Maslow's famous hierarchy of needs, and Douglas McGregor's Theory X and Theory Y, form part of most managers' development. More recent work on goal-setting and personality types is also appearing in mainstream curricula, and some findings tie in with employers such as Virgin or Southwest Airlines which appear to demonstrate that an enthusiastic, motivated workforce is a key part of succeeding.

One barrier to wider adoption of this thinking is that many managers keep the matter of "employee motivation" locked in a drawer marked "soft issues," to be opened only when business is good and unemployment is low. This can be accompanied by a motivational challenge at a personal level; managers can neglect their own developmental needs, and lose sight of their sense of purpose in working.

This book attempts to illustrate that motivation is now a central managerial issue both for individual managers and for the way in which they run teams.

What is Motivation?

» It is essential but elusive. It exists in unlikely places and can be absent in promising locations.
» Motivation is essential in workplaces because employees are volunteers.
» Definitions of motivation and academic studies into its nature have taken place.
» It remains intangible.

"A man was walking down the street, carrying a heavy stone. A passer-by asked him why. He replied 'I'm a slave; I have to do it; I am ordered to.' Another man was walking down the street carrying a heavy stone and was asked the same question. He replied 'I'm paid to do it; it's heavy work, but it's not a bad job.' A third man was walking down the street, carrying a heavy stone, and was asked why. 'I'm building a cathedral,' he replied."

Anon

Motivation is elusive: it exists in the unlikeliest places; it is absent in the most promising locations. The great Russian writer Fyodor Dostoevsky, in his memoirs as a political prisoner, *The House of the Dead*, noted that the prison laborers in the Siberian camp worked harder when there was some useful purpose to the task; by contrast, when they were asked to break up a wooden barge knowing that the timber would not be used as it was worthless, they went about their work in a lethargic fashion.

Motivation cannot be measured, and cannot easily be viewed. Like quality, it is only understood when experienced. It can cause the most monumental and unlikely human achievements to be consummated; it can bind people together in adversity. Its absence breeds discontentment, disaffection, mutiny, and even revolution. The science of motivation begins where the limits of instruction end; and as human beings, as mostly free animals, are loathe to take instructions, it is a broad area.

It determines why, or even if, we get up in the morning. One supermodel is rumored to have quipped that she "wouldn't get out of bed for less than $10,000 a day." Few people have such leverage when they try to determine the nature of their employment contract, but every employee is, as the contemporary management thinker Lynda Gratton points out, a volunteer. Some discretion over the terms of one's work is not only the reserve of the rich and famous. With the rise of interim management and the "portfolio career" some executives can exercise choice. Skilled employees, too, are often in short supply, and their managers neglect their motivation and well-being at their peril. The loss of one key person can lead to the one service or production error that loses the big contract that sends the company under.

As noted in Chapter 1, research is starting to demonstrate a consistent link between the motivation of the workforce and the success of the company. With increasingly complex tasks in a technological world, and with the worth of most firms tied up in "intangible" matters, this link between motivation and success is set to become stronger.

Motivation therefore matters to the individual in the workplace – Why am I doing this work? How does this fit into my dreams and hopes for life? – and to the manager seeking to get the most out of the team – How can I encourage them to reach these goals and share their information?

This book will chronicle the different approaches to motivation – the different studies aiming to discern the elusive matters that create it.

Unlikely as it may sound, a mathematical formula for motivation has been essayed. In the 1960s the workplace psychologist Victor Vroom postulated that motivation can be quantified as being equal to the strength of preference for some action multiplied by the expectancy that the action will succeed. A similar strand of psychological thinking, known as goal theory, contends that people work best when there is a difficult, but achievable, goal. These observations appear to hold in real businesses and in research, but the matter does not end there, because there is more to life and work than goals and expectations. Other dimensions are those of culture and meaning, answering the innate questions that everyone asks of themselves at work: what am I doing this for?

Motivation concerns the incentives which makes people act in a certain way. Companies with effective approaches to motivation seek to synthesize the aims of individual employees with the broader goals of the business. Thus Hewlett-Packard has its "H-P Way," a philosophy of high quality and strong ethics which have seen it through good times and bad; France-based luxury goods group LVMH sees its staff as "ambassadors for the Western way of life." People in the Body Shop want to protect the environment and give a fairer deal to people in economically less developed countries.

There is science in motivation, but there is also a strong school of thought that it is a mistake to pretend that motivation is tangible. It is individual and complex; not formulaic. The ethos, climate, and ethics of an organization, its unwritten rules, matter hugely. A paper produced by the UK-based Industrial Society noted that motivation is difficult to measure, that no satisfactory scales exist, and that some organizations use pay as a motivator, but that this can only be effective in the short term.[1] Yvonne Bennion, a policy director at the Industrial Society, comments: "If the intrinsic caring and nurturing is missing, motivation will be short term. This is particularly so in the current climate of constant change, when more is being left to the line managers to sort out. Many of the issues that matter most lie where people are at the point of work."

Motivation is more accurately described by phrases such as "there was this great buzz," or "the team just gelled," or "we would walk through fire for them," than by dry human resources jargon like competencies or gain-sharing. This does not come easily to managers who are traditionally taught to categorize, to measure, and to budget; nor can it easily be reconciled with market conditions that threaten the income of the organization and the welfare of the employees. In such conflicts lie the difficulties that the quest for motivation faces, as the following chapters attempt to explain.

KEY LEARNING POINTS

» Motivation has an elusive quality and can be a factor even in the most regimented environments.

» Motivation determines why, whether, and how we work. There can be a strong element of control held by skilled individuals as to the terms on which they work and what motivates them to choose an employer.

» Employees are volunteers.

» Research studies show a correlation between motivated staff and business success.

» Definitions of motivation have been set out, and there is psychological theory and research on the subject.

» Despite the science, the subject remains intangible and complex.

» The best companies seek to tie in their broader objectives with the dreams and desires of individual employees and teams. They have an overt culture and sense of meaning as well as a mission statement.

» The nebulous nature of motivation mean that it can in many ways be better articulated through descriptive or metaphorical expressions than through managerial terminology.

NOTE

1 "Management Factsheet: Motivation," The Industrial Society (available to members only).

Evolution of Motivation

» It is difficult to call it evolution as history is littered with setbacks.
» Failures have led to strikes and revolutions.
» Ground-breaking Hawthorne studies in the 1920s started examination of group work, leading to studies on human needs, human drives, personality types, and concepts of achievement.
» The arbitrary divide between "hard" and "soft" business matters has stymied effort.

"Your employees are volunteers."
Lynda Gratton, London Business School professor

It can be misleading to talk about evolution in the matter of human beings' levels of motivation at work. The term evolution means a relentless perfecting of certain attributes to suit needs; it is arguable that finding meaning and motivation in one's work has had as many setbacks as progressive steps in human history. Peaceful trading has been replaced by slavery; craftwork by the assembly line. Recent theories, based on both anthropology and archaeological research, indicate that Stone Age people, far from struggling in squalor and strife, probably worked three or four hours a day in skillful, cooperative teamwork, had a varied diet, and spent the rest of their time devoted to family, religion, dancing, and sex.[1] Is the stressed executive working 70 hours a week, the bored production line worker, or the shanty-town dweller driven out of a shrunken forest and looking for work in the city really enjoying an "evolved" state of affairs?

Despite this, there are positive grounds to believe that lessons are being learned in recent approaches to motivation in management. But it has been a long, bloody, and painful history.

Motivation matters. Poor levels of motivation at work have led directly to the launching of political parties, to strikes, violent confrontations, and even revolution. The work of Karl Marx stemmed from his studies as a young man on the absence of motivation at work, which he and his subsequent followers referred to as "alienation."

Before beginning a history of motivation, a useful reference point can be garnered from one of the more recent teachers. Occupational psychologist Douglas McGregor in the 1950s and 1960s developed the theory that managers tended to subscribe to one of two theories about human nature that determined their approach to the people who report to them. He dubbed these Theory X and Theory Y – concepts which are still taught in MBA courses as well as in the professional development of personnel specialists.

Theory X managers assume that people are lazy, will take a day off sick at the slightest opportunity, and will need to be cajoled, bribed, or forced to do a day's work in the service of their proprietors. Theory X managers instruct. They like pay systems based on a "stick and carrot" principle.

Theory Y managers argue that people want to do well at work, that they seek meaning in their work, and that the key for creativity and high productivity at work is to feed in all employees this need to be involved and have a sense of purpose. Theory Y managers encourage and devolve.

These concepts provide a useful shorthand term for thinkers both before McGregor and since.

The young Karl Marx was, it may surprise some people, a Theory Y man. He was also one of the first serious thinkers to devote considerable attention to the matter of motivation in the workplace, and his verdict on the new factories of the Industrial Revolution was, as history attests, damning. The medieval craftsman, Marx argued, had been in control of his tools and of his work. He took a pride in his craft and the acquisition of skills and experience, and derived self-esteem from such expertise. In the factory, by contrast, the machine was in control of the worker.[2] The individual on the shop floor worked at a rate determined by the speed of the weaving machine or later, in the twentieth century, at the rate of the production line as pioneered by Henry Ford in his car factories. The work was repetitive and tedious. An army of Theory X monitors and assistant managers saw to it that workers did not slack. Even in the more philanthropic enterprises, such as Robert Owen's celebrated New Lanark mills in Scotland in the early nineteenth century, notices in the workplace above each worker symbolized good, bad, or indifferent behavior.[3] The young Marx wanted people to be free of the machine in an imagined utopia that would follow a revolution. The utopia has never materialized, but revolutions have, demonstrating the phenomenal influence of the world of work.

The question of motivation was not seriously picked up again until the work of Elton Mayo in the 1920s. In the first two decades of the twentieth century scientific management had taken the industrial world by storm. It took the principle observed by Marx, of the machine in control of the worker, to new extremes. Henry Ford, in particular, went to great lengths to take all the skill away from the employees, and to limit their input to a robotic, repetitive action in order to speed the assembly line. Employee turnover was so high that in 1914 he doubled wages to $5 a day.

Many industrial employers were disappointed by the returns from scientific management, which often resulted in low morale and strikes. In this context in 1926 the Rockefeller Foundation awarded $100,000 a year for five years to Harvard University to study the reality of working practices and to elicit clues as to environmental or other factors that may boost productivity.

The Harvard researcher heading the study was an Australian psychology professor called Elton Mayo. His work is now legendary. The most celebrated findings came from experiments changing the lighting. Hand-picked groups of workers at Western Electric's Hawthorne plant in Illinois were subjected to higher than normal lighting. Productivity went up. Then they were subjected to lower than average lighting. Productivity went up again. It dawned on researchers that it was the act of treating people as being in some way special that had the decisive impact, rather than the physical environment. This revelation laid the ground for what became known as the human relations school of management, and was the start of the uneven progress toward placing the question of motivation center stage in management thinking.

More revealing insights came from Mayo's detailed study of a group of workers in the wiring bank of the factory. He examined their actual working practices in detail to determine just to what extent people followed orders in a tightly controlled environment and his astonishing answer was "not at all." This group of relatively junior employees was in complete control of how fast or slow they worked. The group put pressure on new employees against working too hard, "rate-busting," or too slowly, "chiselling." There was an established pecking order, and there were cliques, with clique members covering for one another.[4]

The most devastating critique of the Theory X approach came shortly before the term was even invented. Such is the categorization of management thinking that the thinker, a quiet, eccentric American called W. Edwards Deming, is normally bracketed with strategic thinkers and even scientific management. He is known as the father of the quality movement. But he was also an uncompromising critic of the "command and control" approach to management. For Deming quality was not a target to be set from on high, but was the natural effect of removing fear and encouraging teamwork. Motivation was not simply a way, but *the* way, to guarantee quality. Fear, he argued, invites mistakes because errors go unreported.[5]

In the 1930s Deming had gathered a wealth of statistical data on productivity and quality and he concluded, rather as Mayo would have predicted, that Theory X approaches, based on exhortations, targets, management by objectives were counter-productive. His teaching has been closely associated with the dramatic rise of Japanese manufacturers in the 1970s and 1980s.

In the separation of human relations theories from general management approaches, Deming was pigeon-holed into the latter camp, at least in the Anglo-Saxon world, presumably because he was not a psychologist. Therefore his call for "quality" in production found an audience, but his teaching on motivation was given less prominence.

This division of management into two camps remains common, as revealed in the description by contemporary managers of "soft" skills (motivation) as distinct from "hard" skills (finance and strategy). Even Douglas McGregor himself, in encouraging his Theory Y model, called his book *The Human Side of Enterprise*, hinting surreally at the existence of a "side" of organizations – presumably the strategic management side – that somehow did not involve human beings.

McGregor was heavily influenced by Abraham Maslow, the existentialist psychologist. Maslow is most famous for his hierarchical pyramid of needs, from basic physiological requirements like food and shelter to self-actualization.[6] It may seem rather abstract, and removed from work, but Maslow's theory, and McGregor's interpretation of it for managers, dealt with a real problem manifested in staff turnover, low morale, and strike action.

Together with a third psychologist of the mid-twentieth century, Frederick Herzberg, these remain the most influential thinkers on motivating employees in the workplace.

Maslow taught that humans will naturally seek to fulfill their higher needs, firstly for self-esteem, then for self-expression and fulfillment, once their basic material and social needs are met. There was an important distinction between the more basic needs and self-actualization, because with regards to the latter a person will not easily be satisfied, there will be a relentless yearning for more; indeed awakening a desire for self-actualization tends to feed yet more desire for growth.

There have been critics of the hierarchy as being rather formulaic. Do the apparently "self-actualizing" creation of works of art by penniless individuals and even concentration camp inmates not prove that this urge is present even when "lower" needs are not met? Such criticisms are fair, but arguably not significant. The fact that the hierarchy is not rigidly obeyed does not weaken the insight that Maslow had into the significance of aspiration and creativity. Paradoxically it actually strengthens the relevance of self-actualization, as it indicates that fulfillment is a desire for everyone. In 1972 the psychologist Clayton Alderfer proposed a more fluid arrangement of needs (see **ERG (Existence, relatedness, and growth)** Glossary, Chapter 8).

In the 1950s and early 1960s McGregor argued that Maslow's work had major implications for the way in which work is designed and managers manage. His and Maslow's theories represented a serious challenge to the prevailing assumption that poor behavior or morale was caused by the workers'' lack of work ethic or the unions, rather than by poor job design.

McGregor was not neutral in his description of Theory X and Theory Y. He argued passionately in favor of Theory Y.[7] He did not, however, underestimate the difficulty in introducing such participatory managerial approaches, particularly in mass production operations where there was often distrust between managers and junior staff.

The task involves engaging the employee in explaining the purpose of an action, who will then exert self-direction to do the work better than when carrying out an order the purpose of which the employee did not understand. This linking of the aims of the organization and motivational approaches has been the hallmark of successful approaches in companies, even in unpromising situations, as the case studies in Chapter 7 illustrate.

McGregor put his theory into practice at a plant, run by consumer goods group Procter & Gamble in Georgia in the 1950s, which he helped set up. It employed self-managing teams and was overtly based on Theory Y principles. It also outperformed other units at the group.

Frederick Herzberg, a contemporary of Maslow, developed a similar distinction between material and spiritual needs. He characterized the meeting of basic needs as "hygiene" factors – company policy, pay, working hours, and so on – and the meeting of higher needs, defined as achievement, recognition, the work itself, responsibility, and advancement, as motivators or satisfiers. Poor hygiene factors could cause de-motivation, but their improvement did little to add to motivation, he argued.

Another strand of thinking has looked at needs determined by learned behavior and personality. Psychologists distinguish these as intrinsic factors, as opposed to the extrinsic matters of job design and environment examined by Herzberg and Maslow. David McLelland in the post-war years grouped primary needs into three (achievement, power, and affiliation), arguing that different personality types tended to seek one of the three. These ideas will be described more fully in Chapter 8 (see **Achievement**, Glossary).

The most famous theory of personality type is that produced by the Cambridge University professor Meredith Belbin, with his nine archetypes of human personality, described more fully in Chapter 6 (see also **Belbin tests**, Glossary, Chapter 8). This has proved exceptionally popular on management courses.

So why has this wealth of knowledge on how people can be motivated not manifested itself in the emergence of thousands of dynamic, self-managing teams earning exceptional profits? Why is work often boring?

There are probably two main problems: an overly deterministic, scientific approach; and the split between human relations schools of thought and general management.

NOT A PRECISE SCIENCE

There has sometimes been an unspoken assumption that motivation is a discrete science; that introducing motivational idea A to work-force B will produce productivity improvement C. The difficulties with treating it in this way include the near-infinite number of the variables and their intangible nature. There is also the imprecision of the categories. Take "salary." Most would interpret Maslow's and Herzberg's theories as placing salary as a basic or hygiene need, but does salary not have something to do with esteem, which Maslow placed higher up the hierarchy? External variables play a part in the significance of salary, such as the cost of living, and how much similar professions are earning. There is also growing awareness that the fairness of pay and other schemes has a major impact on employee performance.

A paper in 1997 produced by the Catholic University of America interpreted data from a study of teachers in Tennessee a few years earlier. Its conclusion was that salary was a stronger motivating factor than many intangible factors.[8]

THEORY X PERSISTS

Theory X approaches have proved resilient; there have been some arguments on its side. To begin with, in the 1960s and 1970s, trade unions included some individuals who were dedicated to destroying capitalist companies, and overthrowing the system they represented. This reached a high pitch in 1968, which saw a wave of anti-capitalist riots, strikes, and demonstrations across the Western world, and most notably in West Germany, France, and the United States. Trotskyist groups were known to target certain industries with the sole intention of infiltrating unions and causing unrest. To managers it did not seem like a good idea to communicate with and devolve to workplaces where such individuals held significant influence. The influence of Karl Marx, studying unmotivated workers a century earlier, had a long reach.

Furthermore it was, and remains, debatable whether everyone wants to be fully involved in their work. Many people's lives are focused on the family and the weekend's activities, and the spell at the workplace is to pay for these – although of course some workplace personality studies have sought to take this into account. Management thinker Charles Handy quoted one worker, reacting to the introduction of human relations practices at his factory, that he had no wish to "bust my ass to be meaningful." He just wanted a pay check for his week's work.[9]

There can be an impressive clarity about a Theory X workplace: lines of responsibility are clear; decision-making processes are unambiguous; responses can be quick without the time spent discussing and winning people over. It does, however, depend upon the workforce remaining happy with the arrangement.

Theory X became resurgent in the late 1980s and early 1990s through the quest for efficiencies in downsizing and business process re-engineering. Yet growth of interest in more participatory styles has developed in parallel.

THE HISTORIC DIVISION AND ATTEMPTS TO HEAL IT

This has led to the typical contemporary problem, which is not that managers tend too much to Theory Y or Theory X, but that they incorporate both approaches simultaneously, owing to the division between strategy and human relations ideas referred to earlier. Thus in the 1990s empowerment and self-directing teams, resolutely Theory Y approaches, have been introduced alongside downsizing and business process re-engineering which, by viewing individuals as cogs in the re-engineered machine, tend toward Theory X.

The unintentional mix of the two emerged in the decade-long Leading Edge longitudinal study into eight multinational companies by the London Business School in the 1990s. It found that progressive human resources (HR) approaches were sometimes stymied by zealous downsizing, which tore up established career paths, and sowed fear in the workplace. This will be explored further in Chapter 6.

There are serious efforts to overcome the historical breach between the human relations school and strategic management, however. HR managers increasingly acknowledge that it is insufficient to blame senior executives for ignoring the "soft" skills; rather it is incumbent on the HR professionals to learn where value is added in the business, so that people are empowered to help add to profits, rather than for the sake of it. Many are learning to make realistic claims for new approaches that may sound scientific, and take into account the full range of variables and their imprecision. At the same time, a new generation of general managers enthusiastically attend group-work seminars or undergo Belbin and Myers-Briggs personality tests to learn how they can achieve the best from their teams.

This slow rapprochement raises the prospect of unleashing the hidden potential of decades of painstaking psychological study into human nature and human potential.

KEY LEARNING POINTS

» The dominant managerial practice in the past century has been "scientific management," which poses severe difficulties for motivational techniques by regarding employees as economic units.

» Political factors, such as the spread of Marxism into trade unions, deterred some managers from devolving power to staff.

» People have aspirations and desires, and this is not lessened by "command and control" management styles. The seminal study illustrating this was the Hawthorne experiment by Harvard professor Elton Mayo in the 1920s.

» The development of Theory X and Theory Y by Douglas McGregor in the 1950s and 1960s was probably the most cogent, and certainly the most widely accepted, description of contrasting managerial styles and assumptions.

» There has been an enormous amount of study into personality and motivation by psychologists in the second half of the twentieth century, which means that most aspects of job satisfaction, absenteeism, group dynamics, or personal motivation have probably already been studied to some degree.

» Motivation is not a discrete science, because it is affected by matters, including strategic management decisions, that are not specifically aimed at changing motivation. The background factors are variable, not constant.

» Management has been split into "soft" matters, which include motivation; and "hard" matters, which concern the accounts and the strategic decisions. This is arbitrary, and remains the biggest obstacle to implementing motivational techniques, as decisions made under the "hard" category can undermine those taken on "soft" issues. The best examples show a combination – that motivational approaches are geared toward organizational aims and making profits, and that strategic decisions include an appreciation of the impact on motivation. There are positive signs that the historic breach is being healed.

TIMELINE

» **1867** – Karl Marx publishes *Das Kapital*. Argues that alienation of workers is inevitable in profit-making organizations.

» **1911** – Frederick Taylor publishes *The Principles of Scientific Management*, probably the most influential managerial work of the twentieth century, which holds that workers are motivated by money and need strict guidance.

» **1926** – Start of the Hawthorne experiments by Elton Mayo, which indicated there was no link between work environment and productivity, and that output is most affected by the way in which a group of staff is treated.

» **1950** – W. Edwards Deming begins lecture series to Tokyo's Industry Club. Japanese manufacturers start to pursue his ideas on motivation and removing fear.

» **1954** – Abraham Maslow publishes *Motivation and Personality*, including the "pyramid of needs," postulating that all people will seek higher self esteem, and then self-actualization, once basic needs are met.

» **1959** – Frederick Herzberg publishes *The Motivation to Work*, defining "hygiene" factors and motivational factors.

» **1960** – Douglas McGregor unveils Theory X and Theory Y.

» **1968** – *Harvard Business Review* publishes "One more time: how do you motivate employees?" by Herzberg, which ultimately reaches over one million reprints, the journal's most popular article ever.

» **1986** – W. Edwards Deming publishes *Out of the Crisis*, as the West starts to learn lessons from Japan, but motivational matters are hidden by parallel rise of business process re-engineering.

» **Early 1990s** – Intangible assets overtake tangible assets in valuation of companies.

» **1993** – *Team Roles at Work* published by Meredith Belbin.

» **1996** – The concept of emotional intelligence gains ground in managerial circles with the publication of *Emotional Intelligence* by Daniel Goleman.

» **1999** – Leading Edge study by London Business School indicates conflict between business process re-engineering and motivational initiatives.

NOTES

1 Larsen, Spencer Clark *et al.* (2000) *Skeletons in our Closet.* Princeton University Press, Princeton, NJ; and Donkin, Richard (2001) *Blood Sweat and Tears: the Evolution of Work*. Texere, New York and London.

2 Marx, Karl (1867) *Das Kapital 1.*

3 Donnachie, Ian (1999) *Owen of New Lanark and New Harmony*. Tuckwell, East Lothian.

4 Crainer, Stuart (2000) *Management Century*. Booz-Allen & Hamilton, San Francisco, CA.

5 Edwards Deming, W. (1986) *Out of the Crisis*. Massachusetts Institute of Technology Press, Cambridge, MA.

6 Maslow, Abraham (1954) *Motivation and Personality*. Harper, New York.

7 McGregor, Douglas (1960) *The Human Side of Enterprise*. McGraw-Hill, New York.

8 Gawel, J. (1997) *Herzberg's Theory of Motivation and Maslow's Hierarchy of Needs*. Catholic University of America, Washington, DC.

9 Handy, Charles (1976) *Understanding Organizations*. Penguin, Harmondsworth.

The E-Dimension to Motivation

- » Technology only changes consumers' and employees' lives if enough people want it to.
- » The Internet is bringing down trade barriers and access to markets; motivation and skills of employees are decisive competitively.
- » Automation of personnel administration gives personnel managers more opportunities to work with teams, but risks creating remote relationships.
- » Aspects of new economy culture concern motivation of employees.
- » Case study: goodmigrations.com

"History does not follow the path of opportunities but the path of desires."

Biologist Humberto Mutarana

Technology changes lives. But only if people want it to. This qualification is important, and key to understanding progress. Akio Morita, founder of Sony, used to make inventions not by writing code but by making minute, detailed studies of how people lived their lives. It is observable that when he relinquished direct involvement in product development at the company in the 1980s, Sony seemed to lose its knack of developing a truly radical invention like the Walkman that the world takes to en masse.

However much it seems that machines are in control, they are not, yet the belief that the technology alone holds the key to determining the way people work, buy, and do business is strong. The rise of dotcoms in the late 1990s was accompanied by a belief that the technology was changing the rules of marketing and employee relationships. This is not to say there have been no changes in the new economy; but that they tend to appear where technology makes it easier for people to communicate with each other, or have been unrelated to the technology. The dynamic is still a human one.

One of the most dramatic effects of the Internet has been to open up markets to companies in developing countries. Protectionist barriers are no defence when someone in a rich country can have their software sorted out online by a specialist IT firm in Bangalore. India has been the country to take most advantage of the weakened trade barriers so far, but it will not be the last. As communications and technology become cheap, then the principal – perhaps only – differentiator between competitors is the quality of the people who comprise the firm. This places motivation and the ability of staff at the forefront of business strategy in ways that are only beginning to be felt.

The retrenchment in new economy companies during 2001 has masked this development. Capital was so easy to obtain in the period 1998–2000 for anyone with a new economy idea that it was inevitable that there was over-expansion.

The e-dimension has had two major impacts on approaches to motivation. Firstly it is leading to an automation of nearly all of the routine administrative tasks that personnel departments have traditionally carried out. Secondly the informal atmosphere and low hierarchies that characterized many start-ups have had a perceptible impact on business culture, although this has been tarnished by closures and redundancies.

AUTOMATION OF PERSONNEL ADMINISTRATION

Automation is a double-edged sword. Led by the big multinationals such as BP-Amoco, Procter & Gamble, and IBM, companies are introducing intranet-based personnel records systems where employees enter their own data, which are updated in real time. The official line is that this frees the HR specialists to spend more time with employees, understanding their developmental needs, their team dynamics, and how they can work better together; and to spend more time understanding the strategic needs of the business.

This is undoubtedly an opportunity, but progress is not guaranteed. There is a danger that relationships between employees and their senior managers and personnel departments become virtual, with possibly harmful effects on motivation.

This is a problem that US-based industrial group Parker Hannifin has grappled with. The lesson is that there is a balance to be struck. It is important to distinguish between knowledge-rich functions, like training courses on finance or legislation, for which the intranet is ideally suited; and less tangible matters like helping managers to manage staff or customer service representatives to handle difficult clients. "There will always be a need for face-to-face contact," says Paul Everitt, learning and development manager (Europe) for the group. It is easy to see the potential for over-zealous managers to automate too much, claim cost savings to the bottom line, but end up with staff who feel remote and who want to leave.

The rise of the corporate e-mail has also seen increased concerns over surveillance of staff. Companies argue that their facilities are for carrying out business, not for cyber-flirting or checking sports results, while employees complain of having to carry out some personal business from work because of long hours. The thought that a company is secretly monitoring e-mails could undermine motivation at work just as much as – or perhaps more than – the highly visible overseer in a Victorian factory.

Nonetheless the opportunities are considerable. According to research by the European HR consultancy Job Partners, before automation personnel managers used to spend 80–90% of their time just dealing with paperwork. Julian Kulkarni, cofounder of Job Partners, accepts that personnel managers could hide behind the technology, as they used to hide behind the paperwork, but argues that it is more difficult because information is accessible to a wider range of people in the company. Senior managers can hold the personnel department to account because they will know how many job applicants have applied, what their skills are, and what the qualifications of existing staff are. They will want to know that such human ability is being put to good use.

The analogy increasingly being used is with the growing practice of customer relationship management. Customers are fickle, sophisticated, and they bring in the profits. The same goes for employees. "Employee relationship management" is a term with growing popularity.

IS THERE A NEW CULTURE?

The new economy culture is an intriguing beast. Now that many dotcoms have made redundancies it is tempting to take the rather cynical line that there really was no difference and that the very concept of the new economy was a charade. There was, however, more to the identifiably "new economy" customs than wearing baseball caps, using first names, and being able to bring your dog to work, and some are more established than may be apparent. A strong new economy element has been the importance of strong alliances with suppliers. Dotcoms have generally established long-term partnerships with retailers, distributors, and their PR firms, rather than hold competitive tendering exercises, on the basis that it is in everyone's interest in the supply chain to keep each other in business. This has proved effective, but it is not genuinely new, as it has been a feature of Japanese manufacturers since the 1950s and 1960s.

Nonetheless the dotcoms have probably made the practice more commonplace in Western management. The betting start-up flutter. com, for example, described in the October 2000 issue of *Director*

Journal its relationship with its similarly new advertising firm Hooper Galton as "They trust us; we trust them. We will make them rich if they make us famous."

The principle of joint ownership is also geared toward teamwork and motivation. It is common in new economy companies for everyone to own stock, on the basis that, while everyone is entitled to unequal portions of the "pie" that the wealth created represents (assuming it does create wealth), everyone is committed to making the pie bigger. The model lies somewhere between the conventional capitalist organizational structure and that of the cooperative. As with all aspects of the new economy, some of the enthusiasm has waned with the failure of some dotcoms, but it is noticeable that more conventional firms have been following suit with participative pay schemes. The UK – Swiss inventions company the Generics Group listed in late 2000 with a similar pay scheme to the dotcoms. The express desire behind this is to encourage teamwork, information sharing, and morale. Multinationals such as General Electric, Ericsson, and LVMH have instituted all-employee share schemes.

The distinctively informal atmosphere in new economy companies has doubtlessly attracted some people. There could be some generational factors at work. Those born since The Beatles and before the 1980s, known as Generation X, who started work in large numbers in the past decade, are thought to be unimpressed by hierarchy but can be enthused by the prospect of going to a friendly office, being able to wear casual clothes, and have some say in the direction of the company. The generational impact will be discussed further in Chapter 6. With all such trends comes a health warning. Not everyone is motivated by the same factors, even if they could be grouped within Generation X.

A striking measure of the limited impact of "new economy" attitudes came in a snapshot survey of opinions of US citizens carried out on the Netscape Website in July 2001. It asked browsers to vote on whether they considered it justifiable for employers to monitor employees' use of the Internet in work time. One would expect new economy values of high trust and informality to prompt strong disapproval of any form of monitoring, but in fact the vote was split evenly. The sample was self-selecting, but large (just under 30,000 respondents).

More generally, the integrity and sense of purpose of an organization tends to override more superficial matters like dress code and forms of address, as can be seen in the case studies in Chapter 7.

DEALING WITH THE DOWNTURN

When it came to dealing with the economic downturn in 2000–1, many dotcoms and technology firms seemed to fall back on "old economy," Taylorist approaches. Possibly they were even harsher than most traditional firms as the casual, informal style was extended to a peremptory manner of making people redundant. Most firms had grown rapidly, surviving without any personnel professionals or any systematic approach to matters like pay, disciplinary and grievance procedures, or redundancy. Motivation was based upon shared enterprise, growth, and the promise of getting rich. There was no experience, and no anticipation, of trading in difficult circumstances.

Susan Bloch, head of executive coaching at the Hay Group, comments that many young managers in Californian start-up companies have handled downsizing in an "appalling" fashion. "They had never prepared themselves for it," she says.

> "Employees thought 'I've been working 12 hours a day and then I am literally bundled into an office and given five minutes to clear my desk, for no fraudulent or disobedient behaviour.'
>
> "The rest of the organization is devastated, which reinforces the down-turn, as they see their mates handled badly, but they stay because the job market has turned down. Companies are not working well; people are nervous."

Motivational problems occur in successful new economy companies also. They are not always the same as in traditional firms, but they might be more similar than is initially apparent. Some thinkers argue that both "old" and "new" managers need to learn the lesson that it is people, and motivation, that are the key to success, not the balance sheet, nor the Big Idea, nor the technology. Max Mckeown, founder of consultancy Maverick & Strong, which advises companies on their e-strategies, wrote in *Computer Weekly* in May 2001:

"The companies that do well in the new reality are the ones that create real relationships and communities with their customers and make their lives easier. The human touch is going to come back into fashion as it provides the differentiating factor between products and services.

"Despite advances in artificial intelligence, demonstrated by games like Black & White and Half-Life; and sophisticated natural language expert systems, popularised by search engines like ask.com, computers continue to lack a range of human characteristics that are necessary to delivering effective service.

"This was not helped by the somewhat 'anti-human' prejudice of some of those involved in the dot.com rush who assumed that profits would be higher if real people were reduced to a minimum in the e-commerce transaction."

Mckeown adds that e-customers came onto the Net full of expectations that were not met. They came looking for solutions and found only technology. They desired community and "found only one-click shopping." Too many, he argues, acquired a sinking feeling that they were not "good enough" or "smart enough" to use the Net for shopping.

Only people can understand what other people want. "You also know that only people can come up with killer advances capable of solving difficult, ambiguous problems and leap-frogging the competition," he concludes. "The trick is ensuring that the creativity, humanity, and humor of your people are focused on the lifestyle of the e-customer."

Mckeown cites the example of Xerox, which used an anthropologist instead of a business process re-engineering consultant to look at the work patterns of its field engineers. The company found that the engineers kept two copies of the manual, one pristine, and the other dog eared and annotated with wisdom gained from their experience. The company found that engineers got together informally to swap stories about how to fix problems better. Instead of trying to stop the practice, it supported it with radio headsets to allow permanent chatter between engineers, leading to more machines being fixed and "happier, profitable e-customers."

Maverick & Strong argues that many new economy companies make similar mistakes to those of old economy companies. Traditional managers may have focused too much on the bottom line, ignoring the importance of intangible matters, while new economy companies have placed too much faith in technology and in a marketing idea. The real key to success is in liberating people to serve the customer, including the e-customer. Staff have to want to get up in the morning; want to help each other; want to help the customer. They will not do this if they do not feel motivated.

SUCCESS STORY: GOODMIGRATIONS.COM

The UK-based home-moving service goodmigrations.com perhaps benefited from failing to secure significant venture capital. It was set up by Paul Adams and Kate Faulkner in June 1999, after the two MBA students had won the Imperial College Business Plan of the Year award, and been runners-up in the European Business Plan Competition. The idea was to provide a "one-stop shop" Internet service for people buying and selling houses, particularly in England and Wales, where the process is complex.

The company did not secure any funding for six months, and then it attracted a fairly modest amount – £400,000 (just under $600,000) from business incubator the Ideas Hub – compared to the millions given to many start-ups. A few months later the investment market for dotcoms crashed.

Paul Adams recruited people he knew to provide IT and finance management, and subsequently hired a business manager and an administration assistant, who has subsequently learned programming.

The small team used their limited capital to do customer and industry research, rather than launch an advertising campaign. Kate Faulkner spent seven years in marketing roles at blue-chip clients and is aware that brands cannot be built through advertising alone. They decided to drop ambitions to create a consumer brand, and drop the national property database, and instead concentrate on creating an interactive guide to help customers. This tool enables the users to have customised advice, cost calculations, and continually updated information on how their deal is progressing. It is not easy to copy, says Ms Faulkner, which means that goodmigrations.com has been able to sell it under licence to mortgage advice firms with a nationally established brand, including Freeserve and FT Your Money; goodmigrations.com moved into profit in March 2001.

The directors of the firm see motivation as stemming from the joint desire to improve people's lives, specific rewards for good work, ability to learn skills, and stock ownership throughout the company. "The over-riding drive among all of us is the sheer determination that home moving should not be stressful," says sales and marketing director Kate Faulkner. "The business model has changed drastically since we first started, but one piece of continuity is that in one way, shape or form we are going to help improve the home-moving process."

Another motivating factor is the ability for everyone to have a say in the direction of the company, owing to the flatter hierarchy of a new economy firm. This is not common to all small companies, as many are run by the one or two people who founded them and who own all the shares and make all the decisions.

There is also a strong emphasis on encouraging individual achievement and learning. For example a staff member who joined on a temporary contract as an administrative assistant has learned to write code and design a part of the Website.

The goodmigrations.com team gelled, and was if anything pulled together by the challenges of limited capital. There was initial jealousy of other dotcoms attracting millions in funding, but this has turned to a sense of achievement as some of those have since collapsed.

The team feel that they have achieved something; there is already a workable product that has been purchased by large companies and is helping consumers. In doing so the team has learned new skills. Even if the firm did go under, they would walk away with those achievements.

The company has changed its strategy to fit the overriding purpose of the organization. It is this continuing sense of meaning – the desire to make ordinary people's lives less stressful – that is the constant business goal and the key to motivating the team.

KEY LEARNING POINTS

» Technology only changes consumers' and employees' lives if enough people want it to.

» The Internet is bringing down trade barriers and access to markets; motivation and skills of employees are decisive competitively.

» Automation of personnel administration gives personnel managers more opportunities to work with teams, but risks creating remote relationships.

» Aspects of the new economy culture concern motivation of employees, partly through a newly informal atmosphere, and partly through employee share ownership. But some dotcoms have been prone to the "hire and fire" approach.

» Motivational problems in new economy companies can arise when too much is expected of new technology or the new idea. The imperative to motivate teams to serve customers is just as strong in new as in old economy firms.

» Work has to have meaning. Strategy should serve the overriding purpose of the business, rather than the other way around; and staff need to identify with that purpose.

Globalization

» Cultural differences are profound and are something of which most people are unconscious.

» The key to overcoming the problems is to accept that other people's norms and values have validity, and that there may be something unique that that difference can offer.

» There is an emerging theoretical framework for analyzing cultural differences which has been used to help real teams.

» Case study: BP-Amoco.

"We all live under the same sky, but we don't have the same horizon."

Konrad Adenauer

Globalization causes problems for motivation, and it is not a problem of scale. Our cultural hearts beat to different rhythms, but they are like the rhythm of the real heart – so familiar and silent that they pass unnoticed. What is neutral or normal in one culture appears eccentric to an outsider.

The differences concern large matters as well as small: they include one's view on authority, on the nature of time, on conflict, and on showing emotions. This cannot be reduced to regional generalizations. Bolivians differ from Peruvians; Indians from Bangladeshis; the French from the Belgians. Similarities can cross continents also: Japanese businessmen and the upper-class English share a certain reserve; the Irish can feel at home in Cuba. If there were a multitude of variables in motivational theories pertaining to a particular workforce in one culture, this would become multiplied in global companies. The history of a country has a tremendous, silent influence on the present day. Young countries like Israel and Pakistan seem to have a creative, but nervous, energy; republics are distinctive from monarchies; religious and educational systems have a tremendous bearing on people's attitudes to work and to authority.

The unconscious nature of culture has a particularly strong bearing on the world of management because of the dominance in management theories of just one – the Anglo-Saxon. It can be difficult for managers from this background, who wield authority in the world's largest corporations, to appreciate that some of their most basic assumptions are culturally bound, and are not universal. The most dramatic example of this was their difficulty in spotting the rise of Japanese and Korean manufacturers in the latter part of the twentieth century. It is probable that the Anglo-Saxon tendency to compartmentalize business disciplines led managers to misinterpret the theory of total quality, as set out by W. Edwards Deming (ironically, an American), and that the more integrative approach of managers in the Far East gave them an advantage (see Chapter 3 and Deming, Chapter 8).

The strength of cultural differences poses particular challenges for multinational companies. Many have sought to move away from the "colonial" model, in which control and orders are the preserve of a tiny few in the head office, and to give some autonomy to national and regional offices; and to recruit locally. This process can only go so far in a company with a strong desire to maintain the consistency of its services and its brand. Can a company originating in one country be said to have a single culture when its employees come from dozens of different nations? How can cross-cultural teams be motivated?

THE CULTURAL PROBLEMS PRESENTED

Cross-border mergers face particularly strong challenges. Given that they can fail owing to the clashing cultures of different organizations within the same country, the difficulties of a cross-border acquisition are immense. To take some recent examples, it is increasingly felt that the problems encountered by German motor manufacturers in merging with Rover in the UK and Chrysler in the United States owe much to unexpectedly strong clashes of management style and assumptions.

Peter Martin, writing in the *Financial Times*, June 2, 2001, noted that there is a particularly poor record of European firms taking over North American ones. He commented:

> "US management culture is extremely powerful. It is inculcated in the country's excellent business schools, and reinforced by a business publishing industry that endlessly recycles the values and principles of the best companies. This makes it very hard for overseas acquirers to superimpose their own culture."

An example of the sort of problems that can occur can be viewed in the hypothetical case of a meeting of a team comprising a US, a Chilean, and a French manager who are tasked with improving the product knowledge of salespeople around the world. The North American proposes contacting the IT department for a summary of the knowledge held by all the 150 salespeople in the world, with a detailed breakdown by individual, by country, by product type, and to follow up this research with an analysis of competencies and a training program to improve them. The Chilean says: why bother with all these statistics when it is obvious from our last sales meeting that the team lack morale? There is no collective sense of purpose; we need a get-together so that people can enthuse one another. To the North American, a meeting is just an excuse for waffle instead of programmed action. The French team member, on the other hand, is likely to play devil's advocate, challenging the intellectual basis of both approaches in a manner that seems confrontational, something which the other two regard as an irritating distraction.

Language can be a problem even if individuals speak a second language fluently or if there are interpreters, because the precise cultural nuance can be distinct from the dictionary definition. In the example above the Chilean, when talking about the sense of common purpose among the sales team, would at some stage, in his or her own tongue, almost certainly use the term *solidaridad*. In South American Spanish *solidaridad* means teamwork or joint endeavor. But translated into English this typically becomes "solidarity," which in North America means class struggle.

It is easy to see how such a team can descend into mutual recriminations and mistrust. A wise chairperson can point out that the distinct approaches are culturally formed; in reality no one is attacking anyone else personally. Moreover, approaches advocated do not conflict with one another – the competency database can be formed side by side with a morale-boosting seminar, and the French team member can be responsible for putting the results together and providing the framework. The lingual nuances can be tidied up.

TOOLS FOR BRIDGING THE CULTURAL DIVIDE

This is the sort of work that a fledgling consultancy industry would provide to international companies. It builds on a growing body of intellectual research into the particular application of cultural differences in the workplace.

In the early 1990s the Dutch professor Geert Hofstede carried out a comprehensive study of individual employees of IBM in 50 countries, and of three multi-country groups in the corporation. He asked questions about people's views on authority; how they viewed the relationship between themselves and society; how they saw the roles of men and women; and how they dealt with conflict.

Hofstede grouped cultural dimensions into four:

» **Large versus small distance to power**. Those with a large distance to power are people in hierarchical societies, where they feel unable or unwilling to say that they do not agree with the boss. Countries with a large distance to power were found to be Malaysia, Guatemala, and Panama; those with a low distance were Israel, Denmark, and New Zealand.

» **Collective versus individualistic**. Societies with a strong collective culture will feature strong social networks such as the family, while an individualistic society will value freedom and personal choice. The most collective countries in the Hofstede study were Ecuador and Guatemala, and the individualistic nations were the United States and Australia.

» **Masculinity versus femininity**. Hofstede defined a masculine society as one of distinct roles, where men pursue income, recognition, and promotion, while women are oriented toward family, society, and quality of life. The most masculine nations were Japan, Venezuela, and Austria; the most feminine Sweden and the Netherlands.

» **Risk avoidance versus risk taking**. This concerns the extent to which people feel threatened if they take risks at work. Countries with a high risk-avoidance culture will want a set of rules and to play safe. Greece and Portugal topped the list in the study, while Jamaica and Singapore were the most comfortable with risk.

In a similar vein is the work of another Dutchman, Fons Trompenaars, who has analyzed how different cultures view time, nature, and relationships.

On the question of time, he argues that cultures have different perceptions. In North America and northern Europe time is thought to be linear, marked by discrete events, whereas many other cultures see time as circular. On nature he has chronicled differences between nations on whether we should use it or respect it; another way of distinguishing on this matter is whether people feel in control of their destinies or have a sense of fate.

Differing perceptions of social relationships are the cause of diversity across a wide range of matters, Trompenaars has concluded. For example, in some cultures it is encouraged to show emotions openly; in others not. In some countries the family and other collective groups are strong, while other nations are individualistic. Trompenaars described seven perceptual topics where differences were strong and culturally defined. These are:

» relationships and rules;
» group versus individual;
» feelings and relationships;
» how far we become involved;
» how we accord status;
» how we manage time; and
» how we relate to nature.

Both Hofstede and Trompenaars have set up consultancies to help businesses motivate international teams. They are ITIM and Trompenaars Hampden-Turner Inter-cultural Management Consulting. Other agencies include Transnational Management Associates and Psychological Consultancy Limited.

One point stressed by all experienced advisers on the matter is that one's cultural profile does not determine one's ability to understand another culture or work in a multiracial team. What does matter is the concept that other ways of looking at fundamental issues like relationships, time, the purpose of the organization, are culturally rooted and are valid. There is a paradox: by de-personalizing the matter – saying that a certain reaction is culturally bound, not personal – one can achieve better interpersonal relationships. Trompenaars defines this as the ability to reconcile contrasting values, irrespective of the value base one is coming from. He tests for it through competency tests and finds a correlation between high scores and ability to manage international teams.

The most common situation is with a North American company expanding overseas. The ethos of the company is characterized by achievement, growth, results, the spur of competition, the bottom line, and rewards for hard work. To the managers such features are taken for granted, and the values they reflect are taken to be universal. What other way of running a company could there be?

Trompenaars Hampden-Turner Consulting enables a browser to draw up a personal cultural profile online, and offers the chance to test one's judgment on a real case. The case concerns a US electronics company starting to manufacture in South Korea. After a few years margins came under pressure due to competition from Thailand and Vietnam. The firm flew in experienced managers from the United States who imposed a continual improvement program and told the Korean managers to "get their act together." They were given six months to improve results, and bonuses would be awarded for reaching targets. There was no improvement, and after six months another manager flew in with the same, equally ineffective message.

The key to the misunderstanding lay in the failure to appreciate the Korean culture, where status is important. A more effective approach, according to Trompenaars Hampden-Turner Consulting, is to hold out the promise of promotion as a key part of the incentive for improvement, as bonuses in themselves mean much less to Korean than to North American managers.

Whether the Internet will gradually bring about a single world culture is a matter of speculation. The early indications are that it is unlikely. Cultural norms and ways of behaving are deeply ingrained. There is at least the possibility that they will actually be strengthened by the spread of information devices and the adoption of English as a universal language, as people look to preserve their heritage. In Europe, for example, ancient kingdoms such as Scotland and Croatia are re-finding their independence. Culture is part of our identity. Advisers helping multinational firms with their cross-cultural teams seem to have a secure future.

CASE STUDY: BP-AMOCO

Shortly before it merged with the British oil giant BP in 1998, the US Amoco Corporation used Fons Trompenaars' and Charles Hampden-Turner's cultural analysis to help the company with its international management.

Specifically Bill Clover, learning and development services manager of Amoco, employed Trompenaars' and Hampden-Turner's concept of dilemmas in a year-long education program. The consultants' definition of dilemmas and the application to work with managers teases out the conflicts which are culturally formed.

The following four core dilemmas surfaced:

» short-termism vs. long-term thinking;
» empowerment vs. command-and-control leadership;
» individualism vs. team play;
» centralization vs. devolution.

Many of the preferences on these four continua are culturally determined, and by setting them out in this way managers were better able to see that different preferences are of equal validity. Trompenaars and Hampden-Turner have found that the managers who can reconcile opposing values in a diverse organization are the best performers and are most able to motivate their staff.

The four areas of dilemmas that were established tend to be issues that cannot be solved once and for all, but instead must be managed and reconciled over time, says Clover. They are continually changing as the business meets new challenges.

The approach was introduced to Amoco's top 3,500 people worldwide. The company reported a positive response, saying that managers were equipped to look for other ways to approach the issues at hand.

In late 1997 Trompenaars addressed senior managers at the company and explained the theory about reconciliation of different approaches and how the best global managers were able to do this. For example, on the question of universalism versus particularism – either having a preference for a belief in universal laws, or in treating each case as a particular, singular example – Anglo-Saxons tend toward universalism and Asian managers toward particularism. But there are many exceptions within both these groups, Trompenaars and Hampden-Turner state. More importantly, it is not the case that someone toward one end of the spectrum is less able to manage a diverse workforce; what matters is that they are able to understand other people's orientation.

Amoco has since merged with BP, but the concept of underlying cultural values, dilemmas, and reconciliation has "moved us closer to the goal of helping middle and senior managers to see the world differently and behave effectively," says Clover.

KEY LEARNING POINTS

» Cultural differences are something of which most people are unconscious.
» Differences are deeply rooted in how we see ourselves, relationships, the law, and even the passage of time.
» The problems emerging in multinational teams can therefore be profound, and can even wreck mergers and alliances.
» The key to overcoming the problems is to accept that other people's norms and values have validity, and that there may be something unique that that difference can offer.
» There is an emerging theoretical framework for analyzing cultural differences which has been used to help real teams.

The State of the Art

» Most workplaces do not appear to be motivating, because companies often have a confusing mix of motivating and de-motivating decisions.
» Downsizing has a powerful negative effect on motivation.
» Motivation is an empirical science. It will never be possible to isolate and measure all the variables and all the effects.
» Theory has developed into looking at personality types, culture, and the role of goal-setting. There is some correlation with practice.
» Motivational ideas have reached the mainstream.

"Purpose has replaced strategy."
Concetta Lanciaux, executive vice-president human resources,
LVMH

BARRIERS TO IMPLEMENTATION

An unnamed French civil servant is rumored to have quipped once that: "This is all very well in practice, but will it work in theory?" Motivation works both ways, but remains low on the agenda of management teaching.

There is now a wealth of psychological theory on what motivates employees, backed up by anthropological research on what motivates different peoples. In addition, there is a growing body of research evidence that motivating employees is the key to succeeding in business (see Chapter 1 and "Links between motivation and the bottom line" in Chapter 9). Some of the most enterprising managers have put these principles into practice with or without knowing the theories (see the case studies in Chapter 7).

Despite this, much workplace organization seems designed to kill motivation. Call centers set quotas for the minimum number of calls taken per hour; factory workers have to put their hands up to go to the toilet; and employers set up elaborate systems to spy on their staff to check on how many personal e-mails are sent in company time, and monitor the content. Workers buy the bitingly satirical Dilbert books on the absurdities of corporate thinking in their millions, while contributing anecdotes on workplace bullying to Websites such as toxicboss.com. New technology companies making redundancies after the tap of easy capital was turned off in 2000 were just as prone to dismissing people in a harsh and sudden manner as any others, as explored in Chapter 4.

Lynda Gratton, professor at the London Business School and one of the principal contemporary thinkers on workplace motivation, says workplaces should offer meaning to employees and recommends that they overcome fear. In this she echoes and develops theories put forward by W. Edwards Deming half a century earlier. Why are they so often ignored?

In Chapter 3, it was noted that the HR school of management thinking has run on separate lines from the strategic management school, and that while the hope is that they support one another, in practice they can be in conflict. Strategy is not the opposite of motivation; indeed having a sense of direction helps. But much strategic management thinking does not question the still-powerful ideas of Frederick Taylor, which assume that workers are unthinking conscripts who ought to do the top executives' bidding and who are only motivated by money. These powerful assumptions can work against programs aimed at helping motivation that the personnel department might introduce, although they are starting to come under serious scrutiny from management thinkers, as will be discussed toward the end of this chapter.

The unintentional mix of Theory X, treating workers as reluctant conscripts, and Theory Y, treating them as enthusiastic contributors (see Chapter 3), is illustrated in the decade-long Leading Edge longitudinal study into eight multinational companies by the London Business School. Professor Lynda Gratton, who has headed the research, has found that performance in the workplace, and employee morale, sometimes fell during a time when the HR department felt it had introduced more progressive policies aimed at boosting motivation, and aligning the interests of employees with the business goals. The HR policies at all eight companies were pretty much the same. "If you wrote them on blank cards and shuffled them up, it would be impossible to tell which was which," she told the 1999 ECA International Directors Forum. Yet morale and performance differed starkly between the eight firms.

The explanation, she found, was that setbacks had occurred in workplaces that had been characterized by excessive job losses and removal of strata from the hierarchy, which disrupted people's anticipated career paths and sowed the seeds of uncertainty and fear.[1]

The impact of downsizing was pertinent in the early 1990s, and has become a pressing issue again since the shedding of jobs in the telecoms and manufacturing sectors in 2001. Those who are left in the company after the downsizing could perform much worse than before, because they feel guilty at having survived, or feel fearful that they are to follow. This emerges in the Leading Edge research mentioned above, and also in research by the UK-based Roffey Park Management Institute and by Cranfield University.[2]

Other research by Roffey has indicated that mergers can have similarly disruptive effects on people's career prospects and feelings of well-being.[3]

THE SIGNIFICANCE OF FEAR

Recent studies on the impact of redundancy programs indicate a strength and a limitation of psychological theories discussed in Chapter 3, and cataloged in Chapter 8. Highlighting and analyzing human needs and drives has equipped managers with some useful tools in considering human motivation.

But placing human needs on a grid or in a hierarchy gives the impression that all needs are roughly equal, and can be considered separately from matters of strategy. In the peculiar and often intense environment of the factory, office, call center, or retail outlet, where one spends most of one's time at an activity that is vital for one's very well-being, it is likely that some needs are more dominant than others. Deming focused on fear. Now this can be found in any of the theories. In Abraham Maslow's hierarchy it is present as a desire to fulfill the need of safety; and also of belonging. David McLelland referred to the desire for affiliation (see Chapter 3 and Glossary, Chapter 8).

Deming, however, argued that overcoming fear was primary, even dominant, in many workplaces. Fear of the overbearing boss, of missing promotion, of unemployment and being unable to feed one's family, can be felt hour by hour in many real working situations. His arguments paved the way for the dramatic rise of Japanese manufacturing. On a smaller scale they can be illustrated in the work of the US consultant Brad Hill, a Deming disciple, in his high-energy study of medium-sized enterprises featured in Chapter 7.

Both Brad Hill and Lynda Gratton argue that there are no shortcuts to motivating staff, and that employees' fears, resistance, even cynicism, can be entrenched and can exist for good reasons. They can be exacerbated by a restructuring program which appears logical to senior managers.

Many workplaces are constantly changing environments as markets and management teams change. This probably explains the difficulty in demonstrating neat cause and effect formulas in psychological studies. Matters are often artificially assumed to be benign and stable in the world of psychological workplace theory. For example, in a review of 58 articles in five journals, M.B. Arthur and D.M. Rousseau in 1996 found that 74% of the articles on careers assumed environmental stability, 76% had an intra-firm focus, and 81% had hierarchical assumptions.[4]

Despite this, there is a wealth of data which does shed some light on the relationships between some of the different variables. In particular, there are some interesting findings in the field of goal-setting, as shall be explored later.

AN EMPIRICAL SCIENCE

Employee motivation is scientific, but it is a broad, empirical science which considers all matters in the round. It is not a narrow discipline where consistent causes and effects can be demonstrated on discrete matters like conditions, pay, job security, or workload.

Another study, by C.A.L. Pearson, showed better performance by a group of railway track maintenance staff involved in participative goal-setting than in a control group under more conventional supervision.[5] Such attempts at establishing broad principles of trust and involvement on a collective level seem more predictive of success than attempts at micro-analyzing details of conditions and individual levels of job satisfaction.

The Leading Edge study of the 1990s, like the Hawthorne experiments in the 1920s, shows that motivation is not something that can be drafted in a personnel laboratory and introduced to the workplace. It is something that is influenced by all the decisions made by management, not just those made when they are wearing a motivational hat. It is affected by downsizing, union de-recognition, the formation of teams, restructuring, outsourcing, cost-saving gimmicks, and the quality of coffee in the canteen. It can be weakened or destroyed by the presence of a single bully in the management team (or in some cases, in the union).

In a similar vein Duncan Brown of the consultancy Towers Perrin, who is a leading authority on pay schemes, criticizes the formulaic approach to introducing new pay schemes. Managers in many companies that he has advised have tended to assume that there is a "black box" process to be discovered, "with X element of business strategy or core values necessarily leading to Y change in reward practice."[6]

Real workplaces are more complex. In one example that he cites a pharmaceutical company wanted to introduce a team bonus scheme, so as to reinforce a core value of the organization. But it transpired that the team structure was highly fluid, with the membership of teams changing constantly. A team bonus scheme would have created incentives to stop moving between teams, even though this was what the organization needed.

More generally, employers tend to think that the company obeys Newtonian mechanics, Brown adds in *Reward Strategies*, whereas in practice it tends to feature "change-indigestion, overworked line managers, suspicious and cynical staff and truculent trade unions ... No wonder two-thirds of companies admit to problems in implementing their reward strategies."

Successful approaches to motivation have tended to focus on synthesizing the needs of individuals and of the organization as a whole. Meaning is sought in what it is that the company and the workers actually do, rather than in extra-curricular activities such as weekends away or pep talks (although group activities can be used effectively) for teams who are understaffed and who know that work is piling up for them at their desks while they are away.

The better approaches neither pretend that the pay scheme can solve everything nor ignore the importance of income to people's sense of well-being and esteem.

Above all, effective approaches are based on the principles of inclusiveness – treating the organization as a community, fairness, and honesty in communication.

LEADERSHIP

Managers nowadays place increasing emphasis on the concept of being an "employer of choice," or the "employer brand," or exercising motivational leadership, making employees ambassadors for the company.

Leadership is increasingly thought to hold some clues, according to Susan Bloch, the head of executive coaching at Hay Group, one of the world's leading HR consultancies. She reports some interesting developments, with global companies recognizing that the way in which managers manage people and develop teams is of crucial importance.

"We have done a lot of research which is based on what makes an inspirational leader, and what makes the climate and the mood that people feel energised to work in," says Bloch. "A key difference comes down to whether staff think 'Oh God, the boss is in!', versus 'Isn't it great! He or she is here!'," she adds.

What some business leaders are recognizing is that the key lies in the way in which individual line managers manage their people, not in the formal HR processes adopted, nor in the organizational structures. "What I am finding is that big global clients are starting to invest a huge amount of time and energy and money into ensuring that their key people act as coaches, instead of them telling and doing," says Bloch.

Some companies have switched from measuring their managers against performance on the profit/loss account to gauging their impact by asking their staff how they feel about working for their boss, and how they function as a team. So the firm will carry out a survey of employees' attitudes and use this to measure how well their line manager is performing. What also emerges from Hay's work is that managers need a range of styles. There are occasions when they have to be decisive, and others when they have to be nurturing. Some of the matters that employees most value are openness and some honest feedback on their performance. They do not wish to be told that everything is fine when it is not. Everyone knows that employment security cannot come with guarantees, but what de-motivates many teams is being kept in the dark, or witnessing the shabby treatment of a colleague who did not deserve it (see step 6 in Chapter 10).

NEW TRENDS IN MOTIVATIONAL THEORY

While pragmatic learning on motivation has been developing, this does not mean that the wealth of research and theory in psychology has been purely academic. Maslow, McGregor, Herzberg, and others brought intellectual respectability to the matter of human motivation at work, and their theories form part of most courses in general management as well as personnel management. This means that even if a manager does not cite a particular academic guru as inspiration for motivational techniques – or use terminology such as self-actualization or "hygiene factors" – he or she may still have been operating under their benign influence.

Theory itself has moved on. The significance of meaning is reflected academically in the study of goals. Generally, in more recent study, concepts of goals and of personality types have tended to replace the focus on general human needs set out by Herzberg and Maslow.

The seminal work on goal-setting, *Organizational Behaviour and Human Performance*, published in 1968 by E.A. Locke, looked at the significance of the difficulty and specificity of goals that a working team may be set. Locke proposed that employees need clarity about their sense of purpose, and that they need stretching. A meta-analysis in 1987 of research studies on goal-setting bears this out – that it can be effective to set goals for a workforce that are specific and difficult, rather than giving them general "just do your best" instructions.[7] This actually supports the elegant model known as the arousal/performance theory, developed nearly a century ago by the psychologists Robert Yerkes and John Dodson in 1908 (see the Glossary, Chapter 8).

On personality questions, it is well understood that different people are motivated in different ways. Groupings into "types" will always be subjective, even contentious, but those arranging such courses point out that without such training most people will assume that others are motivated in the same way as them, and will experience frustration when they discover that they are not. Helen Fisher, director of the business psychology consultancy Nicholson McBride, says that personality tests should not be used in a dogmatic way, nor for recruitment, but that:

"If you take them with a pinch of salt they are useful as promoters of discussion; they can draw out whether someone is motivated by getting it right or motivated by reaching a goal. The broader issue is that different people have different styles."

At Cranfield University in the UK senior executive managers are taught how to "increase their personal power" in a course that is based on Jungian, Freudian, and Kleinian psychoanalysis. Based on a theory known as the Centaur model it argues that individuals are shaped by their early experiences and that these influence the way in which they are motivated. Some have a need for independence and creativity; others want to express an innate sense of duty; others wish to exercise power – a drive that can be harnessed positively or harmfully. The motivated team will allow people to be true to themselves – self-actualized in Maslow's terminology.

In a similar vein is the ever-popular Belbin categorization of personality types. As a theoretical, diagnostic tool looking at individuals, this may initially appear to be of indirect relevance to motivation. What it does demonstrate, however, together with psychoanalytical studies, is the great diversity of human behavior, and the legitimacy of placing certain characteristics into groups. In lay terms, what motivates some people will turn others off; and Meredith Belbin has produced a model that has helped working teams understand that acknowledging their differences can gain the most out of the strengths of each. A description of Belbin's nine personality types can be found in the Glossary in Chapter 8.

Such tools can help the individual with career choices as well. It can be a revelation, for example, to learn that one is best motivated by an individual achievement and finds group work difficult, and that there is nothing wrong with this. This can be the spur to a successful freelance career, overcoming the negative impression one can have by judging oneself "not good enough" for working in teams or in a hierarchy. The most important motivational ingredient for the individual is, perhaps, the job itself.

Similar models to the Belbin test looking at racial and cultural differences, developed by consultancies such as Trompenaars Hampden-Turner and TMA, were discussed in Chapter 5.

The question of culture raises difficulties for the use of any such test, however. As the designers of TMA's cultural grid themselves acknowledge, slicing up human attributes into neat categories can be said to be symptomatic of an Anglo-Saxon way of thinking, and most tests are designed by Anglo-Saxons, or at least by people having grown up in a predominantly Anglo-Saxon society. In the case of personality tests, while every attribute, such as introversion or sociability, is ostensibly assumed to be of equal merit, it is difficult for those reading the results of such tests to overcome their cultural preferences for certain traits. Hence they can be difficult to implement in multicultural societies and in international organizations. This was discussed in Chapter 5.

EMOTIONAL INTELLIGENCE

There are particularly strong cultural dimensions to interpretation of another key idea that has emerged in recent years in the English-speaking world, which is that of emotional intelligence. In its definition as being aware of the social dimension, of empathy, and of communication abilities, it is arguably the case that Anglo-Saxons are the least "emotionally intelligent" race – which is possibly why they needed to discover it – although this of course is a generalization. Certainly according to the consultancy TMA referred to earlier, people in the UK, North America, and Australia tend to categorize, look at the short term and have a rational ethos. Great care needs to be taken in introducing the idea. It could be that managers in other cultures are highly "emotionally intelligent" already, and that going further in the same direction is not the priority.

It is debatable as to whether "emotional intelligence" is really new – given the similarities with the insights of Mayo and Deming several decades ago – and whether the world of management really needs yet more terminology. Nonetheless there is no doubting the resonance of emotional intelligence with many students and managers, and it will speak to some more than others as a way of re-humanizing workplace relationships.

More generally, this raises the matter of whether the English-speaking countries will continue to be the cradle of motivational ideas. Japanese manufacturers fashioned their own approach to motivation in the late twentieth century, developing a different interpretation of Deming, with considerable success for many years. Asian and Latin cultures tend to look more holistically at problems, and given that a weakness in management application has been the separation of strategy and motivational matters, it could be that they will produce the next great theorists.

GENERATIONAL THEORIES

There are generational theories also. People dubbed "Generation X," born between the early 1960s and early 1980s (precise dates differ according to the theorist), have been entering the workplace in large numbers in recent years. They seem to be characterized by a non-affiliation toward established institutions and social classes – people who would rather volunteer than vote. They are more likely than those born earlier to seek meaning in their work, rather than in political parties or trade unionism.

Concetta Lanciaux, executive vice-president of France-based luxury goods group LVMH, says that in her encounters with young people they are not primarily interested in money. Pay ought to be good, but this is a given – it is not enough for them, she says (see the case study in Chapter 7). They want meaning, and above all a chance for expression and self-development, in their work.

There is some research to back this up. In July 2001 the organization World at Work, formerly the American Compensation Association, asked members, who are compensation and benefits specialists, to list their favorite non-cash benefits. "Opportunity for professional development and skills enhancements" came top, cited by nearly one-third of respondents. Promotion opportunities, a more traditional incentive, was in fifth place, mentioned by just 9%.

Highly skilled, highly mobile individuals, particularly in the richer economies, operate like individual businesses, selling their services not necessarily to the highest bidder, but to the one who offers the most across a range of factors, such as identity, scope for growth and learning, and income as well. The rise of the "portfolio career" was first identified by the management thinker Charles Handy, whose portrayals of individual business people in *The New Alchemists* offer insights into individual motivation.

REACHING THE MAINSTREAM

The keenness of interest in ideas like leadership, emotional intelligence, and Generation X at management conferences does indicate that the matter of staff motivation has moved out of the psychological laboratory and personnel handbook and into the mainstream of management thinking. This is true also of the many managers who display an aversion to these theories but strive to get the best out of their staff in more pragmatic ways.

Motivation is recognized by many business leaders as the ingredient that distinguishes exceptional performance from ordinary performance. It is probable that many managers pay only lip-service to the task of motivating "their most precious asset," but good practice is following in the slipstream of the rhetoric, as we demonstrate in Chapter 7.

Employees are demonstrably the principal resource of most firms, particularly in the service sector, to the extent of forming around 90% of the market value of a company. Talent and skills make up the bulk of a company; the fixed assets comprise only between around 4% and 25% in a modern multinational company.[8] A contemporary company primarily is its people, so how to get the best out of them is, or at least ought to be, the primary business objective. Failing to engage employees' hearts and minds is not a rational course of action.

There is increasing managerial and academic interest in firms which are characterized by high levels of enthusiasm among their staff. They have some features of the "new economy," such as informal dress, first-name terms, and so on, but they are in mainstream services and in some cases are well established. The most famous are Virgin, Southwest Airlines, Ben & Jerry's Ice Cream, The Body Shop, and easyJet. There is an IT training company in London called Happy Computers where, as the name suggests, the staff are encouraged to be joyful as much as possible. Rather than sharing a certain business model or set of processes, the common point among these firms seems to be the energy and motivation of the staff. But they attract attention not only because people working there seem to be having fun, but because they are commercially successful. Southwest Airlines, for example, has had 25 years of continuous profitability and has never had a strike, which marks it out as unusual in the North American airline industry.

Together with the more successful high-tech firms of Silicon Valley, Silicon Fen, Bangalore, and elsewhere, these firms represent the best of the "new economy." Now the new economy cannot stay new, by definition. But this does not mean it will go the way of a temporary fad; the other possibility is that it becomes the mainstream – that the focus on people and motivation replaces the focus on costs and processes as a core strategic discipline.

One of the most influential management gurus currently on the conference circuit, Peter Senge, seeks to invert the traditional managerial focus on fixed assets and money. "A lot of people believe that the purpose of the enterprise is to maximise the return of the invested capital," he told the Hay international conference in Florence, Italy, in

May 2001. "It is a formula for mediocrity. I have never been around a company with a financially superior performance that believes that. Invariably they have different core beliefs – they believe they are there to make the world a better place."

This is not the "soft," aspirational rhetoric it appears, when one considers the success of the high-energy companies listed above. Moreover, Senge is listened to. His books sell in the thousands – to mainstream executives, as well as personnel managers; he is a conference speaker in heavy demand. This is the difference with earlier decades. Senge's inspirational call for meaning and motivation, his discussion of environmental challenges and Confucian teaching, are allowable subjects for senior managers. It is no longer a fringe issue.

He continues: "Work has to have meaning for people and you cannot compensate for that with money." At the intellectual and the pragmatic level, the days of "rational economic man" beloved of Frederick Taylor seem to be numbered.

KEY LEARNING POINTS

» Motivational theory and practice appear to have progressed rapidly in recent decades, but most workplaces do not appear to be motivating.

» Companies often have a confusing mix of motivating and de-motivating decisions taken, due to the split between the HR school and strategic management thinking, and due to the still-powerful influence of scientific management.

» Downsizing has a powerful negative effect on motivation that still appears to be underestimated by managers. Some new studies underline this, and point to fear in the workplace as the dominant de-motivating factor.

» Psychological theories have equipped managers with ways of looking at human drives and needs, but have a tendency to assume all needs are equally present, and to minimize the importance of external variables and the changing environment in real workplaces.

» Motivation is an empirical science. It will never be possible to isolate and measure all the variables and all the effects.

» Leadership is increasingly taken seriously by employers, and managers are sometimes judged by people management ability as well as by financial results.

» Theory has developed into looking at personality types, culture, and the role of goal-setting. There is some correlation with practice.

» The job itself – the career choice – is probably the most important motivational aspect for the individual.

» Ideas around motivation require particular care when translating from one culture to another. New concepts of looking at the organization as a whole, rather than compartmentalizing, may mean that the English-speaking world will cease to be the source of most theories.

» Motivational ideas have reached the mainstream. Added to the academic theories is the fact that people and skills now make up the bulk of value of an organization. There are highly visible and successful companies, like Southwest Airlines and Virgin, that place a high priority on motivation and meaning.

» There is the real possibility that motivation will replace cost control as a major strategic concern.

NOTES

1 Gratton, L. *et al.* (1999) *Strategic Human Resource Management*. Oxford University Press, Oxford.

2 Holbeche, Linda (1997) *Career Management in Flatter Structures*. Butterworth – Heinemann, Oxford; and Sahdev, Kusum *et al.* (2001) *Creating a Resilient Workforce*. Cranfield University/Pearson, Harlow.

3 Garrow, Valerie *et al.* (2000) *Strategic Alliances – Getting the People Bit Right*. Roffey Park.

4 Arthur, M.B. and Rousseau, D.M. (1996) *The Boundaryless Career*. Oxford University Press, Oxford; and *Journal of Management*, May 1999.

5 Pearson, C.A.L. (1987) "Railway track maintenance gangs." *Human Relations*, **40**(6), 473.

6 Brown, D. (2001) *Reward Strategies*. Chartered Institute of Personnel and Development.

7 Mento, A.J. *et al.* (1987) "A meta-analytic study of the effects of goal setting." *Organizational Behavior and Human Decision Processes*, **39**, 52–83.

8 *Measures that Matter*, Ernst & Young, 1997.

In Practice: Success Stories

» Integration of motivational approaches and business strategy: LVMH (France/global)
» Motivation in unpromising places, the work of Brad Hill (USA)
» Democracy and the family in the new economy: Infosys (India).

By way of an introductory note to the case studies, it is necessary to explain the rationale for their selection. The four companies featured below do not represent, necessarily, the four "most motivated" workplaces in the world. Such a selection would be problematic even if an acceptable form of measuring an intangible matter such as motivation were established, given the sheer number of workplaces. Some of the most often cited companies in the context of employee motivation, such as Southwest Airlines, Virgin, or Ben & Jerry's Ice Cream, are not included, not because the author considers them inappropriate – quite the reverse – but rather because they are relatively young companies with a defining ethos and charismatic leadership which are often written about. Most managers work in more conventional firms, and could be forgiven for thinking that colorful "new economy" companies are a case apart, and that motivation does not play a significant business role in firms with a conservative ethos.

Three of the case studies therefore are of companies which are longer established and run along more traditional lines, but which have thought long and hard about the involvement and motivation of employees and sought to improve them, without tearing up the strengths of the founding ethos. This does not deny the existence of achievements and motivation prior to the more recent initiatives; rather it is to signal that such matters have been taken to new levels in workplaces with a long history. Striving for such change is a more typical challenge facing a contemporary manager than those who have a charismatic founder like Richard Branson.

The fourth company, Infosys, could be said to fall into the "new economy" category, but as a firm in the emerging economy of India it brings unique characteristics and insights to bear. As discussed in Chapter 6 ("Emotional intelligence"), the more holistic approach of Asian managers has some advantages over the compartmentalized Western way when it comes to integrating individual and collective motivational needs.

INTEGRATION OF MOTIVATIONAL APPROACHES AND BUSINESS STRATEGY: LVMH

France-based luxury goods group LVMH, or Louis Vuitton Moet Hennessy, aims to apply the concept of quality to everything that it does, from making its famous champagnes to the way it organizes and cleans the offices. It has successfully grown and absorbed smaller firms through acquisitions; it has launched and rejuvenated its products and its image.

Its rise has accompanied the leadership of Bernard Arnault, chairman and chief executive officer since 1985. Arnault is known as a tough negotiator and deal-maker, but another side to his personality is his devotion to recruiting and developing talented people and teams. LVMH is an acquisitive company, but has a policy of zero redundancies when it takes over a firm.

Arnault has been assiduous in recruitment and development since before it was fashionable and, like Bill Gates of Microsoft, has always spent much time directly in the recruitment of key managers and other personnel. In 1999 he set up a management development center, LVMH House, in central London, dedicated to training and knowledge sharing. The most recent annual report includes a whole section on HR, rather than the customary token sentence to be found in many annual reports. It links strategy to development of people. "The group has focused its strategy on doubling its earnings within the next five years; this growth is expected to be driven by recruitment and personnel development," it says.

"If you want to do quality products you have to have quality in everything," says executive HR vice-president Concetta Lanciaux.

"You have to give people opportunities, you have to encourage craftsmanship. People have to feel motivated; to feel that their role is important; that they are not just instruments, they really are actors. They are as important as the product that we produce."

"We have a culture of non-acceptance of imperfection for the products we sell. There is no area of what we do where that is not important. Purpose has replaced strategy in business. To beat L'Oreal no longer motivates people. We now ask them to be ambassadors for Western lifestyle to the entire world. People are motivated by the purpose and not just by beating the competitor.

"If you are able to give people a sense of mission, not just beating the competition, then you have gained a tremendous competitive advantage."

Ms Lanciaux, who is a regular conference speaker, says that when she meets young, aspiring executives and recent graduates and asks them what their goals are, it is noticeable that money and advancement are far from the only matters. She argues that these two issues were dominant motivating forces 20 or 30 years ago but that now people will look for a sense of meaning and for continuous challenge and development as individuals. There is a generational change. People expect good pay, but it is a given, she says, and job satisfaction based on a range of factors is the important priority.

People increasingly want to feel a sense of ownership of a project, and to work internationally. To this end personnel professionals at LVMH maintain a "ready-to-move" list, through which employees can move between different units, broadening their experience.

Rather than be guided by the bottom line the company focuses at least as much on what people do, trusting that if it gets motivation and skills right, the financial results will take care of themselves. "You focus on the processes and also on the results on the same level. Then it is a case of educating people and motivating them. You tolerate error. If people are motivated they bring results anyway," says Ms Lanciaux. "We do give hundreds of employee benefits [but] you can give all the benefits you want, they won't stay just for that."

The company uses the legal requirement in France to make an annual social report, *le bilan social* – which sets out conditions of employees, skills levels, training requirements, and so on – to give itself a measure of the intangible assets that are dominant in a market with high added value and strong brands. Tangible costs, such as head-hunters' fees and salary, are generally dwarfed by the contribution a skilled person makes and the scale of loss if that person leaves and another has to be trained to fulfill the role.

LVMH has also planned for the long term. In the late 1980s it began hiring 150 high-caliber graduates for top management development each year, at a time when many companies were moving away from such a practice, but these people are now adding considerable value and are committed. As a result of this policy around 40% of key posts are now filled internally; this helps people bond together and the creation of a culture. In 2000 LVMH hired 350 young graduates of all nationalities.

These broader aspects of HR policy may appear only tangentially relevant to motivation, but they are crucial for making it work. LVMH's mission of being "ambassadors for Western lifestyle" would not work if people were not valued and if their development was not seen as integral to the development of the organization.

The firm makes a distinction between being a good employer and a soft employer. It argues that in management circles there can be a tendency to assume that a company that is not ruthless and heartless is "soft" – or welfare orientated – but indifferent about business results. LVMH argues that there is an alternative to both of these stereotyped approaches. It treats its staff well, but it expects much in return. It selects carefully, sets high standards, and invests in people to meet the standards. This motivates people because they are encouraged to meet targets set in the real world. Like an increasing number of international companies, it offers stock to a broad range of employees.

The five core values of the company are:

» innovation and creativity
» excellence in craftwork
» brand image enhancement
» entrepreneurship
» leadership and aspiring to "be the best."

In July 2001, despite the economic downturn in most of the world, the company recorded a 12% increase in sales for the first half of the year.

Timeline

» **1985** – Appointment of Bernard Arnault as chairman and chief executive.
» **Late 1980s** – Start of recruitment of 150+ graduates a year for schooling in the culture and management.
» **Early 1990s** – Start of acquisition drive; zero-redundancy principle and five core values established.
» **1999** – Establishment of LVMH House in central London, as management training center for the group. It wins an award from the Corporate University Xchange European Excellence Project one year later.
» **2000** – Some 350 graduates are recruited.

» **2000** – Percentage of vacancies filled in-house reaches 36%, which is five times higher than three years earlier.
» **2001** – Increases sales despite economic downturn.

KEY INSIGHTS

» The most senior executive places a high priority on skills and personal development of staff.
» The various training, pay, and communication approaches are based on the same strategy.
» Meaning is sought in the work that people do; the rules and incentives mirror the values of the organization.
» People are encouraged to achieve their ambitions, to relocate, and to seek promotion.
» Senior managers reject the divide between "hard" and "soft" business matters, instead integrating ambitions of individuals with ambitions for the group.

MOTIVATION IN UNPROMISING SETTINGS: THE WORK OF BRAD HILL

Brad Hill of the Hay Group, Chicago, is an unorthodox motivation consultant. He gave up designing reward packages for top earners – "helping the rich get richer," as he puts it – in order to create schemes that put more money – and also more meaning – into the lives of ordinary working people with unglamorous jobs. His achievements are proof that the principles of motivation apply to all workplaces, not just those dealing in advanced technology or luxury goods.

Hill cites just two influences. Unconventionally, but quite logically, he mentions W. Edwards Deming, who wrote of removing fear from the workplace (see Chapter 3). The other is Alfie Kohn, author of *Punished by Reward*, who argues that bad pay systems can actually remove meaning and motivation from employees, by rewarding behavior they feel bad about.

Below are two of Brad Hill's success stories.

Premium Standard Farms

Factory-floor work in Premium Standard Farms, in Missouri, was of such low status that, Hill recalls, when he first toured the place in 1997 the senior manager accompanying him related how it would be educative to take a son of his to see the work people had to do there as a warning of the sort of fate that might befall him if he did badly at school. It is a bacon factory. Jobs entail killing 5,000 large, warm-blooded animals every day and turning the carcasses into meat. But Hill noted that the Premium Standard Farms brand was highly rated in the US domestic market. Some meat-eaters may not like the idea, but their treasured breakfast delicacy relies upon people doing this work. "This is a fabulous product that helps to feed America," he says. "Managers should focus on that and not on the blood and the dirt."

When Hill made his presentation to the senior managers he felt obliged to inform them that their workers made the highest quality meat product in the United States. This was the message they needed to be giving their staff, instead of implying that they were doing low, demeaning work, he argued. Without this sense of purpose it is a laborious and rather violent job, and one that most people want to leave as soon as possible. The senior managers agreed with him, and a pay and motivational program was put into place.

Pay is more important for junior employees than for executives, for the obvious reason that it can make a proportionally bigger difference to their lives. But as Hill designed packages for people like the workers at the company, he noticed that it was a sense of ownership and involvement – as well as the sense of meaning in what they do – that make the crucial difference in how people feel and are motivated. Hill says:

> "In non-executive, non-sales roles the greatest motivation is in attempting to provide a sense of purpose; to connect their job and individual contribution to the business and provide them with a vehicle to provide suggestions, ideas, recommendations on how they can improve the workplace."

> "I go to where there are blue-collar workers; where there is the opportunity for managers to strip them of their dignity; so the motivational aspect is that people have to be connected to the

business. They have to understand where they fit in, in the scheme of things.''

He notes that at Northern Devices, the part of General Electric that made the ignition device for nuclear warheads, there was a rumor among the workforce that half the components were harmless placebos, and that most of the staff hoped that they made the ones that were thrown away.

People are not a means to an end; people are a means in themselves, Hill argues. This is a major change, and a comprehensive, lasting improvement in motivation is a long-term task. Premium Standard Farms is starting the reap the rewards after four years of the plan, with staff turnover down and steady performance improvements. But research by the Hay Group indicates that eight years is needed to transform a non-motivating culture to a motivating one; after around five years typically only two-thirds of the workforce is committed and there is still considerable scepticism in some quarters.

After approval by the board in 1997, Hill set about pulling together a ''design team,'' which is a crew of volunteers representing each department, including administrative and cleaning staff as well as equipment operators. He gave this team a crash course in gain-sharing – which is the reward consultants' term for a pay scheme managed by the team but geared to operational improvements. Then, to lighten the atmosphere and true to his unconventional approach, he taught them juggling. Hill does this with all the teams he works with; the point is that people can learn a new skill at any age.

The design team – comprising relatively junior staff, remember – were charged with deciding how they wanted to measure and reward their performance. The constraint was that the compensation plan had to be self-funding. By 2000, changes in production procedures suggested by employees at Premium Standard Farms were saving up to $300,000 a month, while bonuses for the year topped $1000 per employee. The latest development is that the staff are considering giving part of their bonuses to charity.

Managers at the plant say that, as well as the benefits to the financial returns, they can perceive a higher degree of dignity and self-worth in the employees. A food safety inspector at the plant commented: "Now

I feel that this is my company, too." One can be a vegetarian and see the rationale.

Timeline

» **1997** – Brad Hill visits the farm and says managers should encourage workers to value the service that they provide.
» **1997** – The gain-sharing pay plan is approved. Hill sets up design team, including junior employees.
» **1998** – Benefits begin to be felt in savings and reduced absenteeism.
» **2000** – Savings reach $300,000, yielding $1000 bonuses for staff.

KEY INSIGHTS

» Meaning is sought in the work.
» Employees are involved in designing the pay scheme.
» Sense of ownership, and chance to improve living standards, are key for blue-collar workers.
» Motivational approach sought mutual benefits for managers and junior staff, creating its own momentum.

Kurdziel Iron, Rothbury, Michigan

Like Premium Standard Farms, Kurdziel Iron is a medium-sized company employing workers traditionally known as "blue collar." It is a unionized environment, in an "old economy" industry, factors which many consider to be unconducive to motivational techniques. The firm was founded in 1937 as a white iron foundry. It now produces parts for the heavy equipment and motor industries, employing more than 300 workers.

In the approach to development and involvement of people, however, there are strong resemblances with the approach at the more glamorous LVMH (see above).

To begin with, the firm has implemented a range of HR policies in tandem with one another. It began in July 1998, when it asked the Hay Group, Brad Hill's employer, to carry out an employee attitude survey. This found that a large majority of staff were happy about teamwork and understanding of their roles, but that very few felt they were able to offer contributions and ideas for improvements. Three-quarters had seen no improvement since three years earlier, which was when a new management had taken over. Eight out of ten did not feel that managers listened to their ideas.

The managers established four main aims. They wanted to:

» establish goals for the organization;
» explain to staff the importance of their roles to the company;
» design a norm of acceptable conduct that was higher than the current; and
» develop a consistent interpretation of successful behavior.

They opted for Brad Hill's gain-sharing pay scheme, but this had to be agreed with the union, the Glass Molders and Pottery Makers. The union initially opposed the scheme; it wanted any project restricted to union members and partly designed by the union. After six months of negotiations, in August 1999, agreement was finally reached. Unions agreed that managers could include all staff, but as the design team was open to volunteers union representatives could put their names forward to help plan the scheme. The final design team of 16 people included 5 middle managers and 11 junior staff, including a union representative. Brad Hill worked with the team to design the scheme, which was then approved by senior managers. Savings that arose from suggestions through the plan were divided three ways: 50% were retained by the company; 40% were to be shared among staff through bonuses; and 10% went into a reserve fund to help the company through difficult trading conditions.

In the first quarter of operation at the end of 1999, there were no savings; in the second there were over $330,000 of savings, yielding $132,000 of bonuses to staff. The maximum bonus was $1070. Despite Hill's caution that such schemes take time to produce results, some fairly swift improvements could be seen. Absenteeism dropped from 6.1% per cent of days lost in the first quarter of 1999 to just 3.4% in the same period a year later, which was the second quarter of implementation of the new scheme.

During 2001 economic conditions deteriorated significantly for Kurdziel Iron, but the company, which owns a trading iron firm in

China, has been able to keep more work in the United States as a result of the scheme, which has seen cost per ton of poured iron reduced by $5, and per ton of finished iron by $11.

Kurdziel Iron is a pragmatic company; it does not base its motivational approaches on theory, but on the recognition of the need to engage employees, connect them to the aims of the organization as a whole, and be attractive to potential workers who might otherwise work in less arduous workplaces than a hot, dirty iron factory.

Where it has been effective is in tying programs together, rather than relying on a single item such as pay to improve matters. For example, it has instituted a cross-training program, which has improved worker proficiency and allowed plant floor managers to respond to daily changes on the factory floor, including bottlenecks and shortfalls in production. More imaginatively still, the steel manufacturer teamed with an environmental charity Whitetails to restore and conserve wildlife in the area surrounding the plant. In early 1998, at about the same time that it was introducing Brad Hill's pay scheme, Kurdziel Iron decided to improve the quality of the woods and wetlands surrounding the plant to encourage wildlife. Each year the firm invites schoolchildren to view the wildlife in its grounds.

This has had a direct, positive impact on employee motivation, reports HR director Steve Wenk. "There are very few foundries that have a cold-water trout stream running through their property. Some of the people do fish the creek."

There is more to motivation than psychological theories and employee appraisal schemes.

Timeline

» **1998** – The Hay Group carries out employee attitude survey, giving mixed results.
» **1998** – Kurdziel Iron establishes new principles for motivation of staff and gives go-ahead for gain-sharing plan, initially opposed by union.
» **1998** – Plan to improvement environment surrounding the plant is agreed.
» **1999** – Union agrees to gain-sharing scheme. Design team establish the formula and implement the plan.

» **2000** – First savings for the company appear; workers achieve bonuses. Absenteeism plummets.
» **2001** – Gains more muted as company enters difficult trading conditions, but scheme slashes cost of product and keeps work in the country.

KEY INSIGHTS
» Employee attitude survey can challenge assumptions about progress.
» Clarity of goals established before changes to pay scheme.
» Agreement with union secured, even though difficult.
» Personnel policies are integrated.
» A major indirect factor – the environment surrounding the factory – can boost motivation.

DEMOCRACY AND THE FAMILY IN THE NEW ECONOMY: INFOSYS

The Indian IT company Infosys takes an holistic approach to motivating staff. Founded only 20 years ago in 1981, the company has enjoyed continuous growth and is now a global organization with offices around the world.

Infosys offers a complete range of software and consulting services such as Internet and e-business consulting. It aims to help its clients transform themselves for the new economy by meeting their IT needs.

The company describes its staff as "highly motivated" and believes this has been achieved by focusing on two primary objectives: making Infosys a company employees enjoy working for; and a commitment to wealth creation for both the company and its employees as individuals.

The link between motivation and achieving the company's business goals is a constant theme at Infosys. As board member Srinath Batni puts it:

"Everyone understands that business success is the company's success and in turn is their own success. Also everyone understands that this growth has to be achieved through ethical means. To be world class in whatever we do is the great motivational factor.''

Few who visit Infosys's 50-acre (20-hectare) ''campus'' just outside Bangalore in south India can fail to be struck by the effort the company has made to make itself an attractive employer on a range of fronts. Here some 4600 of Infosys's total staff of around 8000 are based.

Each morning around 4000 of them arrive at the campus on shuttle buses laid on by Infosys from the center of Bangalore. Others drive to the campus, where, from the moment they arrive, they enjoy a host of options for relaxation and entertainment. Staff can eat breakfast or simply pick up a coffee at the campus's spacious food court. Others start the day with a workout at the gym, a sauna, or by taking a dip in the 5000 square foot (470 square meter) swimming pool.

Other employers might fear that creating so many distractions could affect an employee's commitment to the job. Batni says that, on the contrary, Infosys believes the policy actually increases motivation and commitment.

Other activities laid on for Infoscions, as employees like to call themselves, include mini-golf, basketball, and an art gallery, says Batni. All are aimed at helping staff relax during breaks and ensuring optimal motivation levels when they return to their desks.

Making sure staff are focused is also achieved by helping them to deal painlessly with their day-to-day lives. A travel desk will make reservations for staff for both personal and business travel. Chartered accountants come to the campus regularly to help employees fill out their Income Tax returns. There is also an on-site doctor, ATM, and counters for posting letters and making credit card payments.

Back in the office, Batni says staff are motivated by the company's aggressive growth plans ''to constantly strive for higher goals.'' Indeed, Infosys has an impressive track record. In the last five years it has had an annual compounded growth rate of 60%.

In the first half of 2000/2001 sales grew by 111.75% with net profit increasing by 122.30%. The company's business model focuses on building long-term relationships with clients with a significant proportion of revenue coming from repeat business.

To help staff meet the challenges, all new employees undergo a three-month induction program to ensure they have the skills to succeed at the job. After this, continuous upgrading of skills is constantly emphasized and staff have a wide range of learning opportunities. Online tutorials mean learning does not become a casualty of the unpredictable hours Infoscions work. Workshops are used to help them learn new skills and share specialist knowledge. Company-wide seminars are also held for experts – both external as well as internal – to share their experiences with Infosys employees.

Another important motivation tool at Infosys is its leaders. "We believe in walking the talk," says Batni. "The key role models are within the company and senior management serves as role model for the rest of the company."

As part of this policy, senior managers share information with staff and take feedback and suggestions regularly. They stand in the queue for lunch and breakfast like everyone else and play an active part in social events to which employees' families are also invited. As the HR consultants Hewitt Associates have commented, "[At Infosys] there is no hierarchy and everyone is treated and behaves like equals."

In 1999 Infosys took the decision to give stock options to all employees creating 1773 rupee millionaires and 213 dollar millionaires. By July 2001, 83% of staff had taken up this offer. The stock offer plan comes in addition to competitive salaries and a range of other benefits including loans for everything from home purchase to wedding costs. Infosys chairman N.R. Narayanamurthy has explained the stock options for all decision by talking of the need for leadership to create belief among staff in themselves, the organization, and the goals it sets. This belief, he says, comes from trust, especially the trust that "this company is not about making [only] one set of stakeholders better off." Infosys, according to Narayanamurthy, is rare in that wealth creation for both company and its individual employees is a stated objective.

The company appears to have an enviably clear sense of purpose and direction which it has effectively managed to communicate to employees. Value workshops where the company's values and beliefs are discussed is one means by which this is achieved. Everyone you speak to at Infosys talks of "customer delight," the Indian

English phrase for customer satisfaction. What's more, staff understand how they can play their part in this through their own career progression.

Infosys is justifiably widely admired in both India and the wider world. Many have tried to emulate its achievements and policies. Infosys itself says no one model – either Western or Indian – influenced it in developing motivational policies. Nevertheless, the inclusive attitude toward employee's children and spouses in a country in which family is valued above all else is striking. And it seems unlikely that Western employees, accustomed to a greater division between work and home life, would tolerate the pervasive nature of some policies. "The policies have evolved internally taking best practices from leading corporates across the world," adds Batni. "The fundamentals, however, are the company's own – transparency, ethical conduct, customer focus and leadership."

Timeline

» **1981** – Infosys founded on two main principles: creating an enjoyable working environment and wealth sharing.
» **1996** – Grows by 60% in the year. an annual rate sustained for the next five years.
» **1999** – Stocks made available to all employees, creating 213 dollar millionaires.
» **2001** – Stock ownership reaches 83% of staff.

KEY INSIGHTS

» Democratic principles established; managers queue for lunch with staff, share information, and make stock available.
» Clear philosophy and principles established; strong focus on ethics.
» Value workshops offer staff a forum.
» Families are encouraged to take part in social gatherings.
» Leisure facilities are good.

Key Concepts and Thinkers

» Glossary
» Key thinkers.

GLOSSARY

Achievement – The drive to achieve has fascinated many psychologists, and is of obvious appeal to those seeking high performance in the workplace. It was a source of particular fascination to the psychologist David McLelland in the 1950s, who argued that people tend to be driven toward desire for achievement, affiliation, or power. He was particularly intrigued by the matter of achievement, and argued that the desire to achieve is a distinct human motive that varies enormously from individual to individual. People with a high need for achievement tended to set themselves difficult targets, and thrive on the challenge. Such people are most likely to make effective entrepreneurs. McLelland contrasted this with the attitude of gamblers, who set near-impossible goals partly to evade personal responsibility, and conservative individuals who played safe.

Arousal and performance curve – Developed by the theorists Robert Yerkes and John Dodson in 1908, this mathematical curve is analogous to the concept in physics of the point of elasticity. It posits that individuals need to be stretched, but only so far. At low levels of arousal, or stimulus, performance is poor; people are bored. As arousal increases performance also increases until an optimum level is reached. But if arousal continues to increase overload sets in and performance begins to suffer. So the line rises in an approximately proportional fashion, before falling away, forming an inverted U-curve.

Belbin tests – Cambridge professor Meredith Belbin developed a model of personality types, based on individual motivational triggers, designed to help teams allocate roles. Each type has strengths and an "allowable weakness."

The types are as given in Table 8.1.

Belbin tests can now be done online for £25, at www.belbin.com.

Communication – Real success stories in motivation are characterized more by a strong sense of involvement than particular details of the HR scheme (see Chapter 7). They rely upon honest communication between senior managers and the rest of the staff, so that employees know what is expected of them, and ideally what is the more broadly defined usefulness of their contributions.

Table 8.1   Belbin's personality types.

Type	Strengths	Allowable weakness
Shaper	Dynamic, overcomes obstacles	Prone to provocation
Implementer	Disciplined, practical	Inflexible
Completer – finisher	Painstaking, conscientious	Does not delegate
Coordinator	Defines goals, delegates	Can be manipulative
Teamworker	Cooperative, diplomatic	Indecisive
Resource investigator	Explores opportunities and contacts	Over-optimistic
Plant	Creative, unorthodox	Poor communicator
Monitor – evaluator	Strategic, discerning	Lacks drive
Specialist	Single minded, highly skilled	Dwells on technicalities

Emotional intelligence – The latest, big new idea from the world of personnel is certainly related to motivation, if indirectly. The concept has been developed in the past 15 years by John Mayer, a psychologist at New Hampshire University in the United States, and was popularized by Daniel Goleman in his best-selling 1996 book and popular conference speeches. It is based on the notion that to get the most out of their staff managers need to develop "emotional intelligence" qualities, such as empathy, awareness, and listening skills. It is uncertain as to whether "emotional intelligence" is really new. There are strong echoes with the teachings of Elton Mayo and W. Edwards Deming. Nonetheless, as a powerful and popular concept in management circles, it holds the potential to awaken many managers to the need to look at how they relate to people and motivate them.

Employer brand – Many employers unable to offer either riches or a deeper sense of meaning to the work of employees seek to gain identification with the brand. Being seen as a good employer, or "employer of choice" in the preferred terminology, helps attract people to work at the company. See also **Meaning**.

Equity factor – In the 1980s Richard Huseman and John Hatfield developed a concept known as the equity factor. They focused on the nature of a relationship, including an employer employee relationship. They developed three axioms:

» People evaluate their relationships by comparing what they give to a relationship and what they get from it.
» When that which is given to a relationship does not equal what an individual receives, the individual feels distress.
» People who feel distress in relationships because they give more than they get will restore equity.

ERG (Existence, relatedness, and growth) – This was developed by the US psychologist Clayton Alderfer in the early 1970s. It builds on Maslow's theory of a hierarchy of motivational needs, but it argues that needs at different levels can be sought simultaneously, and that there is a fluidity, rather than a step-change from one "level." Alderfer grouped the complex array of needs he identified into three broad groups. Existence is similar to Maslow's basic physical needs, such as food, shelter, and water; relatedness refers to the desire for belonging and social relationships; and growth is similar to Maslow's concepts of esteem and self-actualization.

Ethics – There is a growing body of thought that the purpose and the wider conduct of an organization has an impact on the commitment and performance of its employees. Corporate social responsibility is increasingly felt to have positive effects on the employer as a brand, in attracting people to work for it. Those sceptical about its influence might consider the "dinner party" test: just how proud are you of telling your friends who you work for? See also **Meaning**.

Fear – The subject of fear is covered by psychological theories, although at times only implicitly. Its negative effect was, however, central to the argument of the most influential motivational theorist of the twentieth century, W. Edwards Deming. He argued that fear suppressed the exchange of honest information giving in an organization, because people were scared of giving bad news. By weakening the sense of belonging to an organization, an employee is less likely to give his or her best. Fear is likely to be a dominant factor when there is high unemployment and/or overbearing bosses.

Contemporary management thinker Lynda Gratton similarly argues that fearful employees may choose to withhold knowledge that is useful for the organization. For more on Deming and Gratton see "Key thinkers" below, and Chapter 3.

Feedback – Near the top of the list of most employees' requests in research on motivation is the expressed desire for honest feedback, according to the business psychology consultancy Nicholson McBride, which has carried out such surveys. It argues that anything other than honesty is de-motivating, because it will not be believed. See Chapter 10.

Hawthorne effect – This is named after Western Electric's Hawthorne factory, host in the 1920s to Elton Mayo's experiments on productivity. Mayo found that changes to the physical environment had negligible effect on output, and that beneficial effects were more likely to come from ways in which a team are treated by senior managers. See Chapter 3 and "Key thinkers", below.

Hygiene – This is nothing to do with personal cleanliness, but it does pertain to the environment. The influential thinker Frederick Herzberg developed his theory of hygiene factors and motivator factors in the 1950s. "Hygiene" in this context means matters such as company policy, salary, working hours, and holiday entitlements, and is still used by many HR professionals, particularly in the field of employee relations. They can often cause dissatisfaction, he argued, but high standards in these matters do little to enthuse. Motivation is more likely to be derived from matters concerning the five characteristics he listed: the job itself, achievement, recognition, responsibility, and advancement.

Leadership – According to research by the Hay Group, the climate of an organization is the biggest determinant of employees; motivation; and climate is set by the nature of leadership. See "Leadership" in Chapter 6.

Meaning – Maintaining a sense of purpose to one's work is arguably the most important ingredient to obtaining motivation in the workplace. Few people are motivated by the feeling that their effort is useless; or, worse, that it is aiding objectives that they profoundly disagree with. It can be said to carry more weight even than the job itself. One of the most popular quotes used by motivational professionals to describe this is the probably apocryphal comment of a cleaner at NASA in the 1960s who, upon being asked what her role was, replied "I'm helping to put a man on the moon." Meaning plays a crucial role in the motivation of people in the public sector, although nurses, doctors, fire-fighters, police officers, and social workers have at times argued that taxpayers and politicians take advantage of this and keep wages too low. Few people in the private sector are able to say "I saved someone's life today."

Pay – It is at the peril of any management to ignore something as fundamental as pay when considering how to motivate their staff. As discussed in Chapters 3 and 6, and in the case studies in Chapter 7, pay does not sit neatly tucked away in the "hygiene" category along with working conditions. People do not work only for pay; but they do work for pay. It can represent esteem, social standing, or recognition of achievement, and is generally deeply embedded in the way people think about their work and their employer. See "The work of Brad Hill", Chapter 7; and "Books, articles, and other material" in Chapter 9.

Taylorism – Frederick Taylor, probably the most influential management thinker of the twentieth century, cannot be truly regarded as a major thinker on motivation, as he regarded the matter as a straightforward affair. Nonetheless he had a view on the subject (he had a view on every subject), which was that people are economic creatures who seek to maximize their income and therefore should be cajoled into working hard by the promise of better pay. Managers who are fond of piece rate systems and the less complex forms of performance-related pay are Taylorist in their approach.

Theory X – Defined by Douglas McGregor in the 1950s, this is the set of assumptions held by managers who view employees as reluctant workers, who need forcing or cajoling into work (see "Key thinkers" below, and Chapter 3). Frederick Taylor, arguably the most influential management thinker of the twentieth century, held Theory X values.

Theory Y – Also described by McGregor, this theory holds that people want to work and to be motivated (see "Key thinkers" below, and Chapter 3). W. Edwards Deming, probably the second most influential thinker after Taylor, held Theory Y values.

Theory Z – Douglas McGregor, the inventor of Theory X and Theory Y, was working on Theory Z at the time of his death in 1964. It was a synthesis of X and Y (see below).

Vroom's expectancy theory – In the 1960s the workplace psychologist Victor Vroom postulated that motivation can be quantified as being equal to the strength of preference for some action multiplied by the expectancy that the action will succeed. He also argued that if performance is always rewarded in a certain way the employee will be motivated to perform to the required level.

Work-life balance – A growing awareness that people want more from life than money and advancement has seen the inclusion of work-life balance policies in discussion of motivation; previously it might have been dismissed as a "hygiene" matter. In recent years in high-tech firms, particularly in Silicon Valley before the downturn in 2001, firms were falling over themselves to offer such non-cash perks to help staff stay connected with their families. Those which did not offer reduced hours instead have enabled staff to have free child-minding, or concierge services, or even bring their pet to work.

KEY THINKERS

Meredith Belbin

During the 1970s and 1980s, Cambridge professor Meredith Belbin and his team of researchers based at Henley Management College, UK, studied the behavior of managers from all over the world. Managers taking part in the study underwent several psychometric tests and were put into teams of varying composition, while they were engaged in a complex management exercise. The research team studied their distinct personality traits, intellectual styles, and behaviors which were grouped into 13 "types" under three broad headings (see **Belbin tests**, above). Belbin's easy-to-understand approach has rapidly been adopted by management teams and colleges, and the terms have entered many managers' vocabulary. The HR section of most business teaching will include reference to the categories, and the tests are popular among management teams wishing to get to know one another better. The tests are judged to help motivation by encouraging participants to appreciate that different individuals are motivated in different ways. As an example, someone who is a "completer – finisher" is unlikely to be enthused to do anything other than a tangible task with a deadline.

Key works

Management Teams, Why They Succeed or Fail. Butterworth – Heinemann, Oxford, 1981.
Team Roles at Work. Butterworth – Heinemann, Oxford, 1993.
Changing the Way We Work. Butterworth – Heinemann, Oxford, 1997.
Management Without Power. Butterworth – Heinemann, Oxford, 2001.

W. Edwards Deming

This quiet American, who began his career as a statistician, was probably one of the two or three most influential business thinkers of the past 100 years, along with Frederick Taylor and Peter Drucker. His influence can be seen in the adoption of his practices at Japanese manufacturers which grew rapidly in the post-war years. The nation instituted an annual Deming Prize in his honor.

At the heart of his managerial philosophy is a theory about motivation, although this has not always been fully recognized. Deming argued that motivation and engagement of the workforce is key to producing consistently high-quality products and services, and to do this managers should overcome fear. This was the opposite of the approach of Henry Ford, a disciple of Taylor, who argued that "men work for two reasons: pay and the fear of losing one's job." Deming argued that fear inhibited honest communication, commitment to quality, and creativity. His managerial philosophy was spelled out in 14 steps that ought to be taken. Some of the 14 pertain to strategic management or cost control, but eight are solely or partly about motivation. They are as follows:

» Cease dependence on inspection to achieve quality. Eliminate the need for inspection on a mass basis by building quality into the product in the first place.
» Institute training on the job. This should be a part of everybody's everyday activities.
» Adopt and institute leadership. The aim of supervision should be to help people and machines and gadgets to do a better job. Supervision

of management is in need of overhaul as well as supervision of production workers.

» Drive out fear so that everyone may work effectively for the company because they want it to succeed.

» Break down barriers between staff areas or departments. People in research, design, sales, and production must work as a team, to foresee problems of production and in use that may be encountered with the product or service.

» Eliminate slogans, exhortations, and targets for the workforce asking for zero defects and new levels of productivity. Such exhortations only create adversarial relationships, as the bulk of the causes of low quality and low productivity belong to the system and thus lie beyond the power of the workforce.

» Remove barriers that rob people of pride of workmanship – eliminate the annual rating or merit system.

» Institute a vigorous program of education and self-improvement for everyone. Let them participate to choose the areas of development.

Key works
Out of the Crisis. Massachusetts Institute of Technology Press, Cambridge, MA, 1986.
The New Economics. Massachusetts Institute of Technology Press, Cambridge, MA, 1994.

Lynda Gratton

London Business School professor Lynda Gratton, one of the most popular speakers on the subject of personnel management on the conference circuit, says that motivation and the search for meaning should be at the heart of business strategy, not only HR strategy. A psychologist by training, her doctoral study was on Maslow's hierarchy of needs, and in her corporate and academic life she has expanded on the relevance of human beings' search for meaning and a higher purpose at work. Her 10-year Leading Edge research into multinational firms found that some with identical processes and procedures had widely varying employee commitment and financial performance. The key to exceptional performance lies in a long-term commitment to integrating the aims of the organization with the aims and dreams of individuals, she argues. She cites Hewlett-Packard, with its "HP Way," as one of the few firms to achieve this. She points out that the intangible matters of trust and commitment give Hewlett-Packard an advantage that is difficult or impossible for competitors to imitate, as distinct from patents, capital, or processes. People are not interchangeable parts, she writes, in an implicit criticism of business process re-engineering.

In her most recent work, *Living Strategy*, she puts forward three tenets that all managers ought to recognize as central to management. These are that:

» We operate in time; we have a "memory of the past and of the future." The past is continually with us, as are our dreams for the future. Skills and desired group behavior take years to establish. Current behavior is influenced by what we expect to happen in the future.
» We search for meaning. Unwritten rules in an organization can be more powerful than the overt rules and guidelines. We seek to create meaning from our work, and will work best if we find it.
» We have a soul. We are not machines, programmed to deliver in a rational manner; we have emotions. We can choose to share or withhold our knowledge at work, depending on how we feel.

The problem with many companies is that they pretend that people leave their emotions, dreams, hopes, and fears at home when they come into work. Successful companies like Hewlett-Packard tap into the emotions of their workers and encourage them to express their creativity.

But this takes years, not months, she argues. A successful transformation at Glaxo Pharmaceuticals (part of what is now Glaxo Smithkline Beecham) to motivate staff, and align their interests with those of the group as a whole, took around 12 years, she says. Many companies are trapped into looking at the short term, which can develop into a vicious circle, as companies seek to cut costs to amend for failing to invest in people, and in doing so cause further mistrust.

Key works

Strategic Human Resource Management. Oxford University Press, Oxford, 1999.
Living Strategy. Financial Times Prentice Hall, Harlow, 2000.

Frederick Herzberg

The twin-level theory of motivation developed by Herzberg in the 1950s can be oversimplified and misunderstood. He argued that the core elements of the employment contract and physical environment were "hygiene" factors that did little to motivate directly. Matters such as the job itself and interpersonal relationships were "motivators." Some have questioned whether matters can be so neatly separated (see Chapters 3 and 6), but Herzberg's teaching was that a comprehensive consideration of all aspects of work was necessary, meaning that disagreement over his categorization does not fundamentally affect the wider point. He did not belittle "hygiene" factors.

It has been a common observation by employee relations experts that industrial disputes nearly always concern the "hygiene" factors – or at least appear to. Herzberg's teaching that dissatisfaction is unlikely to be derived solely from the pay scheme or working hours has encouraged managers to look beyond the obvious negotiating points, and consider more subtle matters such as interpersonal relationships. Herzberg has probably helped the move toward partnership in the workplace, away from strikes and brinkmanship.

Key work
The Motivation to Work. F. Herzberg, B. Mausner, and B.B. Snyderman, John Wiley, New York, 1959.

Abraham Maslow

In theoretical terms, Maslow was the most original thinker on motivation in modern times. His famous hierarchy of needs is known by anyone who has studied management, and can be represented as follows:

» Self-actualization
» Esteem needs
» Belonging needs
» Safety needs
» Physiological needs.

Self-actualization is a "being need," i.e. rarely fulfilled; but it is at the pinnacle because it represents the fullest expression of a personality. In keeping with his existentialist spirit, Maslow argued that people will, and should, seek to maximize their talents and be all they can be. The other needs on the hierarchy are "deficit needs," which means that people will be satisfied once they are met before moving on to higher needs. While the strict accuracy of the model has been challenged – it is disputed that people wait for basic needs to be satisfied before seeking fulfillment in others – it is also true that Maslow helped awaken an awareness of the importance of meaning and motivation in all employees (see Chapter 3). His work heavily influenced Lynda Gratton (see above) who talks and writes on the challenges of achieving high performance in modern, complex organizations. Douglas McGregor was also strongly influenced by Maslow.

Key works

Motivation and Personality. Harper and Row, New York, 1954; 2nd edition 1970.
Eupsychian Management. Irwin Dorsey, Ontario, 1965.
Towards a Psychology of Being. John Wiley, New York, 1968.

Elton Mayo

The Australian psychologist Elton Mayo was the pioneer of contemporary approaches to motivation. He brought a scientific rigor to a largely neglected area, at a time, in the 1920s and 1930s, when junior employees were assumed to be unthinking automatons under the strict control of management. His celebrated Hawthorne experiment (see above) opened up the significance of motivation. He made two major breakthroughs: firstly in demonstrating that team dynamics appeared to outweigh the physical environment as an influence on productivity; secondly, that groups set up and obey their own unwritten rules, even in highly regimented workplaces. The conclusion from the research was that the treatment of people was far more important than physical environment. But Mayo also argued that the social world of adults is complex, and primarily focused around work. He said that a complaint is generally not a recitation of fact, but a symptom of underlying discontent. Informal groups and cliques within work tend to hold the decisive influence. Group collaboration does not happen by accident; it has to be planned and developed.

Key work

The Social Problems of an Industrial Civilization. Harvard University Press, Cambridge, MA, 1945.

Douglas McGregor

The inventor of Theory X and Theory Y was a sophisticated thinker, despite the apparent simplicity of the twin categories. His thinking had its roots in the ideas pioneered by Abraham Maslow about human nature, but he tailored his thinking more specifically on the workplace. His definition of Theory X was pertinent as it was – and probably still is – the case that most managers subscribe to a view of employees as needing firm direction, with clear sanctions for misconduct, and bonuses for high productivity. This made his analysis similar to Deming's teaching on the negative consequences of fear, as Theory X managers believe that people are motivated by money or by the fear of losing their livelihood. Theory Y is a very broad category, and McGregor examined many different aspects to the task of taking non-confrontational approaches. He acknowledged the difficulty of establishing Theory Y; for example, he recognized that there are occasions when authority needs to be exercised. He also recognized that a variety of managerial styles was possible within Theory X, and that it was unfair to caricature managers in a "command and control" establishment as being bullies.

Shortly before McGregor died, in 1964, he was answering critics that Theory X and Theory Y should not be seen as mutually exclusive and that the needs of both the individual and the organization should be taken into account. Theory Z was intended to be a synthesis of the earlier two concepts, and in this McGregor was prophetic, as such allying of individual and corporate needs has been a feature of recent success stories (Chapter 7).

Key work

The Human Side of Organizations. McGraw-Hill, New York, 1960.

Resources

» Useful organizations
» Journals
» Books, articles, and other subject matter
» Links between motivation and the bottom line.

USEFUL ORGANIZATIONS

The Hay Group (www.haygroup.com)

The Hay Group is a global people management consultancy, which offers direct advice to companies on pay, motivation, and other aspects of personnel. Its slogan of "People before Strategy" reflects an approach that sees the ways in which people work as the building block of a successful enterprise. It also produces a global compensation database.

Watson Wyatt (www.watsonwyatt.com)

Watson Wyatt brings people management and financial management together in its approach to consulting. It has developed the Human Capital Index, a measure of how well organizations motivate and use people, which it claims is predictive of business success (see **Links between motivation and the bottom line**, below).

Towers Perrin (www.towers.com)

Towers Perrin is adviser to around three-quarters of the world's largest companies, on the subjects of HR management, communication, pay, and organizational effectiveness. It seeks to improve business performance through people.

SHL (www.shlsolutions.com)

SHL, formerly known as Saville and Holdsworth, is an HR consultancy with considerable expertise in selection and recruitment. But it also offers developmental tools, including a cultural audit.

Nicholson McBride (www.nicholson-mcbride.com)

Nicholson McBride is a motivational specialist. It is a business psychology consultancy, whose role is to offer direct advice and help to businesses in teamwork and development of people both on an individual and a collective basis. One of its core areas of expertise is to help businesses recognize and develop their unique culture.

World Federation of Personnel Management Associations (www.wfpma.com)

The WFPMA is a global network of professionals in people management. It was founded in 1976 to aid the development and improve the effectiveness of professional people management all over the world. Its members are predominantly the continental federations which are made up of more than 50 national personnel associations representing over 300,000 people management professionals. Languages on the site are English, German, French, and Spanish. The secretariat is currently the UK's Chartered Institute of Personnel and Development, on www.cipd.co.uk

The Society for Human Resource Management (www.shrm.org)

The Society for Human Resource Management is the voice of the HR profession in the United States. It provides education and information services, conferences and seminars, government and media representation, online services and publications to more than 165,000 professional and student members throughout the world. The Society is the world's largest HR management association.

World at Work (www.worldatwork.org)

World at Work, formerly the American Compensation Association, is a global, not-for-profit professional association of more than 26,000 compensation, benefits, and HR professionals. Founded in 1955, World at Work is dedicated to knowledge leadership in compensation, benefits, and total rewards disciplines associated with attracting, retaining, and motivating employees. In addition to membership, World at Work offers certification and education programs, online information resources, publications, conferences, research, and networking opportunities.

Other useful contacts

» Human Factors International: www.humanfactors.co.uk
» Delta Consultants: www.deltaconsultants.com
» Directory of Business Psychologists (North America): www.business-psychologists.com
» European Network of Organizational and Work Psychologists: www.ucm.es/OTROS/Psyap/enop/index.html
» Links to a range of HR organizations can be found at: www.personnel-today.com/pt_links/links_listnew.asp

JOURNALS

Most national personnel management associations publish journals, see "World Federation of Personnel Management Associations" above. The most appropriate national association can be contacted for more specialist academic journals on employee motivation and psychology in different languages. The Websites under "Other useful contacts" above can also help with this inquiry.

BOOKS, ARTICLES, AND OTHER MATERIAL (BY SUBJECT MATTER)

Cultural work

De Luque, Mary (2000) "The impact of culture on feedback-seeking behavior." *Academy of Management Review*, October.

Hall, Edward (1959) *The Silent Language*. Doubleday, New York.

Hofstede, G. (1990) *Cultures and Organizations: the Software of the Mind*. McGraw-Hill, New York.

Trompenaars, F. and Hampden-Turner, C. (1997) *Riding the Waves of Culture – Understanding Cultural Diversity in Business*. Nicholas Brealey.

Trompenaars, F. and Hampden-Turner, C. (2000) *Building Cross-Cultural Competence*. Yale University Press, New Haven, CT.

Training material on cultural differences: www.euronet.uwe.ac.uk/emas/training/train1-4.htm

Guide to motives, values, and preferences: www.psyconltd.com/mvpi.html

Self-assessment guide: www.thtconsulting.com

Downsizing and restructuring

Garrow, Valerie *et al*. (2000) *Strategic Alliances – Getting the People Bit Right*. Roffey Park.

Holbeche, Linda (1997) *Career Management in Flatter Structures*. Butterworth – Heinemann, Oxford.

Sahdev, Kusum *et al*. (2001) *Creating a Resilient Workforce*. Cranfield University/Pearson, Harlow.

Ethics

Blanchard, H. and Vincent Peale, N. (1988) *The Power of Ethical Management*. William Morrow, New York.

Ferrell, Q.C. *et al.* (1990) *Business Ethics: Ethical Decision-Making and Cases*. Houghton Mifflin, Boston, MA.

Roddick, A. (1991) *Body and Soul – Profits with Principles*. Crown, New York.

Generational theories

Lipsky, David and Abrams, Alexander (1994) *Late Bloomers: Coming of Age in Today's America – The Right Place at the Wrong Time*. Random House, New York.

Rushkoff, Douglas (1994) *The GenX Reader*. Ballantine Books, New York.

Strauss, William and Howe, Neil (1991) *Generations: The History of America's Future*. William Morrow, New York.

"How to" books

Blanchard, H. *et al.* (2001) *The Little Book of Coaching: Motivating People to be Winners*. HarperBusiness, New York.

Bruce, Anne and Pepitone, James (1999) *Motivating Employees*. McGraw-Hill, New York.

Buckingham, Marcus *et al.* (2001) *Now, Discover Your Strengths!* Free Press, New York.

Freemantle, David (2001) *The Stimulus Factor – the New Dimension in Motivation*. FT Prentice Hall, Harlow.

Heller, Robert and Hindle, Tim (1999) *Essential Managers: Motivating People*. DK Publishing, London.

Motivating Employees: Managing Best Practice No 55. Industrial Society, 1999.

Motivational Strategies, *Personnel Management*, ed. K.M. Rowland and G.R. Ferris. Boston: Allyn & Bacon, 1982.

Individual motivation

Arthur, M.B. and Rousseau, D.M. (1996) *The Boundaryless Career*. Oxford University Press, Oxford; and *Journal of Management*, May 1999.

Deci, Edward (1996) *Why We Do What We Do: Understanding Self-Motivation*. Penguin, Harmondsworth.

Handy, Charles (1989) *The Age of Unreason*. Arrow Business Books, London

Landmark works

Edwards Deming, W. (1986) *Out of the Crisis*. MIT Press, Cambridge, MA.

Gratton, Lynda (2000) *Living Strategy*. FT Prentice Hall, Harlow.

Herzberg, F. (1968) "One more time: how do you motivate employees?" *Harvard Business Review*, Jan–Feb.

Marx, Karl (1867) *Das Kapital 1*.

Maslow, A. (1954) *Motivation and Personality*. Harper and Row, New York.

McGregor, D. (1960) *The Human Side of Enterprise*. McGraw-Hill, New York.

Leadership

Cooper, Robert (2001) *The Other 90 Per Cent: How to Unlock Your Vast Untapped Potential for Leadership and Life*. Crown Publishing, New York.

Maister, D. (2001) *Practice What You Preach*. Free Press, New York.

Profile of David Maister: http://www.thetimes.co.uk/article/0,,280-2001243504,00.html

Organizational studies

Handy, C. (1976) *Understanding Organizations*. Penguin, Harmondsworth.

Katz, D. (1964) "The motivational basis of organizational behavior." *Behavioral Science*, **9**, 131–46.

Locke, E.A. (1977) "The myths of behavior modification in organizations." *Academy of Management Review*, **2**, 543–53.

March, J.G. and Simon, H.A. (1958) *Organizations*. John Wiley, New York.

Pay

Armstrong, Michael (1996) *Employee Reward*. Chartered Institute of Personnel and Development.

Bonuses Aren't Just for the Bosses. Fast Company feature on Brad Hill (www.fastcompany.com/online/41/hill.html).

Brown, D. (2001) *Reward Strategies*. Chartered Institute of Personnel and Development.

Koln, Alfie (1999) *Punished By Rewards: The Trouble with Gold Stars, Incentive Plans, A's, Praise and Other Bribes*. Houghton Mifflin, Boston, MA.

Lawler, E.E. (1971) *Pay and Organizational Effectiveness*. McGraw-Hill, New York.

Personality

Belbin, M. (1981) *Management Teams, Why They Succeed or Fail*. Butterworth – Heinemann, Oxford.

Belbin, M. (1993) *Team Roles at Work*. Butterworth – Heinemann, Oxford.

Psychological studies in three parts: need theories, value theories, goal theories

1. Need theories

Alderfer, C. (1972) *Existence Relatedness and Growth*. Free Press, New York.

Bellott, F.K. and Tutor, F.D. (1990) "A challenge to the conventional wisdom of Herzberg and Maslow theories." Paper presented to the Annual Meeting of the Mid-South Educational Research Association, New Orleans, LA.

Gawel, J. (1997) *Herzberg's Theory of Motivation and Maslow's Hierarchy of Needs*. Catholic University of America, Washington, DC.

Herzberg, F. (1966) *Work and the Nature of Man*, World Publishing, Cleveland, OH.

Herzberg, F. *et al.* (1959) *The Motivation to Work*. John Wiley, New York.

Maslow, A. (1954) *Motivation and Personality*. Harper and Rown, New York.

2. Value theories

Adams, J.S. (1965) *Inequity in Social Exchange, Advances in Experimental Social Psychology*, ed. 1. Berkowitz. Academic Press, New York, pp. 267-99.

Deci, Edward (1985) *Intrinsic Motivation and Self-Determination in Human Behavior*. Plenum Publishing, New York.

Dittrich, J.E. and Carrell, M.R. (1979) "Organizational equity perceptions, employee job satisfaction and departmental absence and turnover rates." , *Organizational Behavior and Human Performance*, **24**, 29-40.

Hackman, J.R. and Oldham, G.R. (1976) "Motivation through the design of work: test of a theory." *Organizational Behavior and Human Performance*, **19**, 250-79.

Hatfield, J. and Huseman, R. (1989) *The Equity Factor*. Houghton Mifflin, Boston, MA.

McLelland, D. (1961) *The Achieving Society*. Van Nostrand, New York.

McLelland, D. (1978) "managing motivation to expand human freedom." *American Psychologist*, **33**, 201-10.

Vroom, V. (1964) *Work and Motivation*. John Wiley, New York.

Vroom, V. (1976) *Leadership and Decision-Making*. University of Pittsburgh Press, Pittsburgh, PA.

Weick K.E., Bougan, M.C. and Maruyama, G. (1976) "The equity context." *Organizational Behavior and Human Performance*, **15**, 32-65.

3. Goal theories

Arousal/performance curve: http://www.nwlink.com/~donclark/hrd/history/arousal.html

Bandura, A. (1969) *Principles of Behavior Modification*. Holt, Rinehart & Winston, New York.

Locke, E.A. (1968) "Toward a theory of task motivation and incentives." *Organizational Behavior and Human Performance*, **3**, 157–89.

Mento, A.J. *et al.* (1987) "A meta-analytic study of the effects of goal setting on task performance 1966–1984." *Organizational Behavior and Human Decision Processes*, **39**, 52–83.

Pearson, C.A.L. (1987) "Railway track maintenance gangs." *Human Relations*, **40**(6), 473.

Reiber, S. (2000) Effects of physical working conditions and perceived workload on job satisfaction and intention to leave. MSc Dissertation, Cardiff University.

Satire and dissent (www.toxicboss.com)

Adams, S. (1996) *The Dilbert Principle*. Harper Collins, London.

Adams, S. (1997) *The Dilbert Future*. Harper Collins, London.

LINKS BETWEEN MOTIVATION AND THE BOTTOM LINE

1. London Business School

In the long term, longitudinal, Leading Edge research by the London Business School the companies studied were Hewlett-Packard; Glaxo Pharmaceuticals; Citibank; Lloyds Retail Banking; BT Payphones; Kraft Jacobs Suchard; and WHSmith News.

It was reported that there was serious damage to motivation and to performance in the companies that had more sudden and drastic reorganizations. Employees were confused and uncertain because traditional routes for promotion were torn up and colleagues were made redundant. There was less disruption, and better performance, at Hewlett-Packard and Suchard Jacobs Kraft, where change was less abrupt and integration of people processes into business was ingrained.

Reference

Gratton, L. *et al.* 1999 *Strategic Human Resource Management*. Oxford University Press, Oxford.

2. University of Sheffield; London School of Economics; Chartered Institute of Personnel and Development

This study, published in 1997, based on research into medium-sized manufacturing companies by the Institute of Personnel and Development with the University of Sheffield and the London School of Economics, shows a close correlation between staff commitment and better performance on a range of "hard" measures, including profitability.

Researchers measured the effect of HR practices in the companies, and used the same methodology to measure the impact of technology; strategy; emphasis on quality; and research and development.

HR were by far the most influential, explaining 19% of the variation in profitability compared to research and development which registered 6%, and technology which accounted for just 1%.

Reference

Patterson, M. *et al.* 1997 *Impact of People Management Practices on Business Performance*. Chartered Institute of Personnel and Development.

3. Mark Huselid's work at Rutgers University (http://www.rci.rutgers.edu/~huselid/)

Mark Huselid has been studying the relationship between a company's personnel policies and its business performance for many years. He has found that the firms which make development of their people a fully strategic goal perform spectacularly better than others. Practices that encourage people to behave in a way that supports the organization's goals are effective. But he makes the point that this is a sophisticated task which cannot be achieved through pay systems and new personnel systems. Staff must have a sense that they are valued; pay must reward teamwork and communication as well as ambition.

4. Jeffrey Pfeffer (http://faculty-gsb.stanford.edu/pfeffer/)

Pfeffer is a professor of organizational behavior at Stanford University in California, whose findings are similar to those of Mark Huselid and who, similarly, has studied the relationships between people management and business performance for many years.

His book, *The Human Equation: Building Profits by Putting People First*, argues that people matter because they are the organization and embody its aims. If people are treated well, and are encouraged and helped to develop, they will excel. Companies fail where staff are competing against each other.

5. Watson Wyatt's Human Capital Index (www.watsonwyatt.com)

The international consultancy Watson Wyatt has completed two thorough surveys of HR practices at major companies – one in North America and one in Europe. It concluded that commitment to good practices in employing people adds up to 30% in total return to shareholders over a five-year period.

Not all personnel initiatives were found to be effective. What the research found was that there is a negative impact only where the activity in question is not tied in with the objectives of the firm.

Most of the successful elements feature a high degree of concern for employees' welfare. They are:

» recruiting excellence;
» a collegial, flexible workplace;
» clear pay awards and accountability;
» clear and honest communication; and
» prudent use of resources.

6. The Hay Group: culture change and business performance

This study has focused more on the quality of individual leaders within organizations.

A summary of the findings of the Hay Group research can be found in *People Management*, June, 28, 2001, which is published by the Chartered Institute of Personnel and Development. The author of this article was Chris Watkin of the Hay Group, who can be contacted on chris_watkin@haygroup.com

7. The Gallup Organization
(http://www.gallupjournal.com/GMJarchive/
issue1/2001315i.asp)

The Gallup Organization has carried out some comprehensive question-naire-based surveys in recent years exploring the correlation between employee well-being and profitability. One report on the findings reads:

> "We collected employee engagement scores and business unit outcome data, such as profitability, sales, employee retention, customer satisfaction, for 7,939 business units, teams or work-groups in 36 companies ... The correlation was positive: highly engaged individuals were most often found in the high-performance units."

Ten Steps to Making Motivation Work

» The top team should be on board
» Take culture into account; avoid jargon
» Pay matters
» Don't forget the simple things
» Your staff are not stupid
» Don't forget motivation when cutting costs
» Take care with personality profiles
» The company is a community
» Things can get worse as well as better
» Give feedback: be honest; don't skimp on praise.

1. THE TOP TEAM SHOULD BE ON BOARD

Pull in the top team. This is a strategic matter; motivational approaches fail when pulling in a different direction from the main business goals. Use the research studies in Chapter 9 to show to the boss how motivation makes a difference to the bottom line. Learn how to read the accounts and speak the language of the senior executives. The senior executive team need motivating and developing too; they are employees as well. For those who do have some say in this, it is important to incorporate their approach to teamwork. If you absolutely cannot win the board around, at the very least understand the business objectives. Look at the purpose of the organization and tease out the importance of the service that you provide. Unless you are actually supplying land mines to children, there will be one. This is the key to giving meaning to employees' lives and connecting them with customers.

2. TAKE CULTURE INTO ACCOUNT; AVOID JARGON

All the most experienced advisers concur that the importance of unwritten rules in organizations is underestimated. People in a complex society such as a company or public sector organization will be most motivated if they see the senior managers exhibiting the behavior that they seek to inspire in others, and if the rules reflect the true values of the organization. It is no good having mission statements about "empowering" people if there are strict rules about clocking in and clocking off or producing so many widgets per hour.

Take the cultural dimension into account, especially if you are dealing with a multiracial team. This can be best achieved by calling in one of the specialist advisers (see "Culture," Chapter 9, and "Tools for bridging the cultural divide," Chapter 5). If this is beyond the budget, then at least take time to listen to, and perhaps catalog, the hopes, fears, and expectations of the team you are working with.

Culture is not just a racial issue; different organizations within the same country will have a very different ethos and unwritten rules. IBM, for example, is very different from Ben & Jerry's. A public sector organization has a different culture from most private sector companies. Slavish copying of a procedure from one firm to another can be an error. "Dress-down Fridays," for example, will be motivating in some companies but will cause embarrassment and stress in others.

Avoid jargon. This makes motivation sound remote from people's daily lives and they turn off. Moreover, it often makes little sense to people hearing the message in their second language. Don't say "This is a robust strategy, fit for purpose;" say "We are producing this service because it helps people in their daily lives." Don't say "We have a goal-oriented reward strategy;" say "We want you to work in teams to help provide this important service, and the team will have a shared bonus if you fulfill this achievement."

3. PAY MATTERS

Don't forget the pay system. This cannot solve all problems, but unfair pay can cause serious de-motivation. The important elements in pay are not the minute details of the scheme, or whether it is identical to the one used by BP-Amoco or Microsoft or whichever benchmarked company, but whether the principles of fairness, transparency, and links to the behavior that the company actually wants are there. One of the most serious de-motivating phenomena is the feeling of a grievance. What matters here is the subjective experience; if people feel hard done-by their efforts will drop, and issuing propaganda by telling them, in effect, "You are not that low-paid, really," will be counterproductive.

If people are given some say in the way in which their efforts are rewarded, this can be very effective (see "Motivation in unpromising places", Chapter 7). Similarly, if people feel that they can have a share of rising income, and that their pay and conditions will be the last thing to be cut when conditions are difficult, they are more likely to stay motivated. For a fuller exploration of pay and performance, see also Performance and Reward Management, also in the ExpressExec series.

4. DON'T FORGET THE SIMPLE THINGS

Uncover easily avoidable grievances. They could be laughably easy to correct, such as poor-quality coffee in the vending machines or lights that keep turning themselves off. Do not become frustrated by these grievances; they may seem silly to you but they are important to someone else. In the offices of one publishing company the lights were turned off automatically, four times a day, prompting a drop in the energy of the workers each time they had to get up from their desks and turn the lights back on. Meetings were interrupted; trains of thought were lost; time was wasted. The company was actively de-motivating its staff four times every day, Monday to Friday, 52 weeks a year, by saying "Our electricity bill is more important to us than your welfare and your teamwork."

Frederick Herzberg defined the work environment as a "hygiene" factor. While there is some dispute over definitions, the significance of Herzberg's work lay in his insight that the matters which make people unhappy are not necessarily the opposite of those which make them happy. An ambitious motivational exercise is unlikely ever to move out of square 1 if managers do not first listen to, and remove, basic grievances.

Decisions about the physical environment are often taken with the bottom line costs only in mind, but the way in which they are felt by the rest of the staff is as a statement about them and their welfare. Only if they see their welfare as being the last, and not the first, thing that is cut when savings are being made will there be a chance of trust and motivation between senior managers and the rest of the employees.

5. YOUR STAFF ARE NOT STUPID

Remember that people are intelligent. It is a common misconception that intelligence rises as one goes up the hierarchy. Wrong. If a business does not have a strategy, and if the motivational approaches do not tie in with this, then everyone in the company knows it immediately and cynicism sets in.

"Barriers to implementation" in Chapter 6 explored the common phenomenon of employers whose strategic policies undercut the motivational exercises introduced by the personnel department. Rather than give the impression of a balance between cost-control and creative processes, it often creates the sense that there is no leadership and no direction. Hence the importance of tying in motivational approaches with the aims of the business (see step 1, above).

People work for different reasons. Not everyone wants to devote themselves to the company, but this does not make them bad employees (see "Not a precise science," Chapter 3).

6. DON'T FORGET MOTIVATION WHEN CUTTING COSTS

Maintain a positive approach to motivation during difficult trading conditions. It is more important, not less, at these times, and the teamwork forged during a recession can lay the foundations for more impressive growth when favorable trade returns. Motivation can even be maintained if redundancies are necessary. One novel approach to redundancy was developed in 2001 by telecoms giant Cisco Systems. It offered some staff one-third pay, plus full bonuses including stock options for one year, if they spent that year working for a non-profit organization linked to the firm. Sales manager Peter Santis took up the option to work for a charity that provided Internet access to low-income communities. He told the *Wall Street Journal* (July 23, 2001) "For now I am just happy that I get to do something that motivates me."

In a similar vein the British luxury car manufacturer Rolls-Royce and Bentley kept people at home on full pay in 1997–8, rather than make redundancies, asking them to "bank" their hours for when trade picked up.

These sorts of exercise will help motivation of the staff who remain, who do not want to see former colleagues treated shabbily, as well as helping recruitment when business picks up again. See "Barriers to implementation," Chapter 6.

7. TAKE CARE WITH PERSONALITY PROFILES

Consider carrying out personality profiles of a group using the Belbin test, but make sure you have the time and expert supervision to carry it out properly. A little knowledge in a rushed program is confusing and unhelpful.

From an individual's point of view a test such as the Belbin or Myers-Briggs test can help uncover factors that motivate, and even help guide career decisions. For example, someone who emerges as a teamworker (see Table 8.1, for definition), who has been struggling with a role in authority, might be able to take this as a cue to seek a new career in the caring services, or to be a conciliator or chairperson within the same organization, rather than an authority figure. People have even been known to take considerable pay cuts in order to seek a role that they are more comfortable with.

The benefit to a team in carrying out such an exercise is that people can recognize each others' strengths and permit an "allowable weakness" which can reduce stress and the less realistic expectations.

Another important proviso in any such exercise – and this goes also for team-building days out – is to ensure that work does not pile up at the workplace while people are away. This can be counter-productive.

8. THE COMPANY IS A COMMUNITY

Don't forget the junior staff. The company is a community and all of it can be affected by decisions which directly concern only a few employees. An expensive exercise in motivating highly paid profes-sionals at the same time that the company is laying off hundreds of hourly paid workers will have a negative effect on the motivation of everyone in the organization. Your fired janitor could be the best friend of your star programmer.

Junior staff often stay for many years, and many deal directly with customers. Collectively they can have far more impact on the perfor-mance of the company than the executive team.

The case studies of Kurdziel Iron and Premium Standard Farms in Chapter 7 ("Motivation in unpromising places: the work of Brad Hill") show the positive effects of an integrated approach to business strategy and the different strands of people development and motivation in workplaces featuring hard, unglamorous jobs.

Companies with exciting strategic aims and tasks for the managers, and unremitting, rules-filled jobs for junior employees, can be dysfunc-tional.

The cartoonist Scott Adams reported that one of his readers once e-mailed him with a real example. The reader's employer had "simul-taneously rolled out two new programmes: 1) a random drug testing programme; and 2) an 'individual dignity enhancement' programme."[1] This is the sort of muddled mixture of Theory X and Theory Y that is described in Chapters 3 and 6. The employer simply has not decided whether it regards its staff as empowered volunteers or lowly conscripts to be kept in order.

9. THINGS CAN GET WORSE AS WELL AS BETTER

Don't assume progress will happen. If people object to the motivational exercises, listen respectfully to the complaints. Carry out employee attitude surveys. This can be helpful in a small firm as well as a large enterprise, and it needs to be done anonymously; otherwise people will not fill them in. Believe the results. Don't blame the employees. Moreover, it is essential to act on the results, or people will have expectations raised and will feel disillusioned.

It is a good idea to have, if not regular surveys, then at least a repeat exercise each time that a change in the environment and conditions takes place.

There can be an assumption that motivation increases in proportion to the number and complexity of HR practices introduced. Not only is this not the case, but new measures can actually be counterproductive if people feel disengaged from and somewhat cynical toward senior managers. This is particularly the case if a new exercise is accompanied by a welter of jargon (see step 2, above). The important principles are trust, openness, honesty, and fairness. It is better to have a simple pay system implemented while honoring these principles, rather than a more sophisticated system that is imposed on individuals without consultation, and whose purpose is not fully understood.

10. GIVE FEEDBACK: BE HONEST; DON'T SKIMP ON PRAISE

Feedback to employees forms an essential part of motivation. It is something staff frequently ask for in employee surveys. They want to know how well they are doing in an honest manner. Formulaic responses, especially those of the good news/bad news/good news approach (dubbed the "feedback sandwich") can be dispiriting to hear. If someone has failed, they need to know why and to be equipped to avoid future failure. If they have succeeded, then to be told so will motivate them for months. People love to feel good about their contribution.

In both it is necessary to be specific, not general. In other words, say "The swiftness with which you reassured that client helped secure the contract – well done;" rather than "You're a really valued member of the team, you know.'' Too many managers qualify or hedge praise even when it is amply merited, perhaps for fear that one of their subordinates might be more able than him- or herself, or consider themselves to be.

KEY LEARNING POINTS

» Policies to improve motivation must tie in with the philosophy and objectives of the organization as a whole. Without support from the board they will struggle.

» All policies affect motivation, not just those of the HR department. Strategic decisions and the physical environment are especially important.

» Honest communication is essential at all times, right across the organization. Misleading or patronizing statements, and the withholding of information, are de-motivating.

» Motivation of staff must be a priority when dealing with difficult trading conditions. Staff pay, numbers, and welfare should be seen to be the last area for cutbacks.

» Personality profiles can help with career decisions. They must be taken with care. Work should not be piling up for people while they spend a day or afternoon on personality tests or other motivational exercises.

» Employees thrive on hearing accurate feedback on how they are doing.

NOTE

1 Adams, S. (1997) *The Dilbert Principle*, 2nd edition. Boxtree, London.

Frequently Asked Questions (FAQs)

Q1: Is motivation a personal, individual matter, or does it depend upon team dynamics and leadership?

A: See "The significance of fear," Chapter 6, and "Leadership," Chapter 6.

Q2: Is motivation most relevant to high-energy, new economy companies?

A: See Chapter 7; and "Is there a new culture?", Chapter 4.

Q3: Might the Internet decrease personal contact and reduce motivational approaches?

A: See "The automation of innovation," Chapter 4.

Q4: How can we even think about motivation when we have to cut costs?

A: See "Barriers to motivation," Chapter 6; and step 6, Chapter 10.

Q5: Is it necessary to study psychology before implementing motivational techniques?

A: See "New theories," Chapter 6, "Not a precise science," Chapter 3, and all of Chapter 7.

Q6: We face a militant, obstructive trade union.

A: See ''Motivation in unpromising places,'' Chapter 7.

Q7: We cannot afford to match a competitor's pay rates.

A: See ''Pay matters,'' Chapter 10.

Q8: What do we do if our motivational approaches are out of sync with decisions concerning staffing levels and strategy?

A: See ''The historic division and attempts to heal it,'' Chapter 3, and step 1 in Chapter 10.

Q9: How can we win the senior managers round?

A: See ''Links between motivation and the bottom line,'' Chapter 9.

Q10: How can we motivate a multinational team?

A: See Chapter 5.

Acknowledgments

I am grateful to Helen Fisher, director of Nicholson McBride, and David Ryves, director of the Peachell Group, for their help in compiling the list in Chapter 10.

Acknowledgments are also owed to Louise Rudolph and Anita Cross of the Peachell Group and Dominique Hammond of People Management.

Acknowledgements

Index